Scott Levy asks you to consider and use social media ʝ medium like TV or radio. Instead of channels, there are user projʊᴄₛ. *and posts are the programs, and Levy provides a look into getting loyal viewers to stay tuned. Content matters but Context matters more. Scott hustles and is a true entrepreneur, and if you know me I love hustle!*
—GARY VAYNERCHUK, AUTHOR OF *JAB JAB JAB RIGHT HOOK*

As an actress in Hollywood I thought I had a pretty good grasp of the importance of social media and its uses. Then I met Scott Levy from Fuel Online and he opened up a whole new twitterverse to me! He taught me so much about Twitter and Facebook and the power they have in my career. Thanks Scott. Wait, I should tweet this . . .
—REBECCA MADER, ACTRESS,
LOST, DEVIL WEARS PRADA, IRON MAN 3

Scott and Fuel Online are a top-notch firm. They know their business inside and out and are continually focused on delivering results. I'd highly recommend them
—MIKE HOSTETLER, FOUNDER AND CEO, APPENDTO

Fuel Online has been an awesome addition to our social media team and has provided us with great insight and fresh ideas in the field. Scott and his team at Fuel are easy to work with and get things done the right way.
—RONNIE WINTER, CEO/MANAGER/LEAD SINGER THE RED JUMPSUIT APPARATUS

If you want to go far, you need the fuel. If you want to rock social media, you need Scott's book. He takes all the crap we hear on a regular basis and turns it into actual facts you can put toward increasing your business and revenue TODAY. Want to make sense of it all? Buy this book.

—Peter Shankman Founder, HARO (helpareporter.com) Co-Founder, Shankman | Honig (shankmanhonig.com)

There are very few good starting points for knowledge when it comes to figuring out how to work your way through the world of social media. As I read Levy's tips, I found myself nodding in agreement several times—as though I could've written them myself based on my own experiences. I'd have no need to write them now, though—I'd simply share this book!

—Chris Pirillo, Social Content Curator LockerGnome.com @ChrisPirillo

I'm impressed with the work of Scott Levy of Fuel Online. Scott not only truly understands social media engagement, but he's one of Kred's top influencers. To really understand influencers, it is important to be one as well.

—Andrew Grill, CEO, KRED a leading social influencer platform

Scott Levy and Fuel Online consulted in my social media strategy. I found his advice helpful as we brainstormed together on Twitter. He helped me with my Facebook presence as well. He's been in the business a long time and knows his stuff.

—Todd Hoffman, Creator, *Gold Rush* on the Discovery Channel

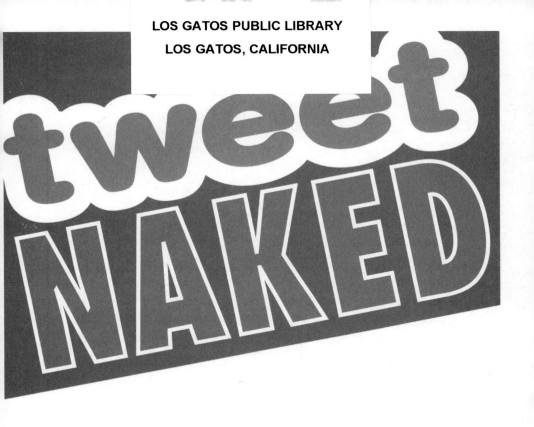

tweet NAKED

Scott Levy

a bare-all **SOCIAL MEDIA** strategy
for boosting your brand and your business

Entrepreneur
PRESS®

Publisher: Entrepreneur Press
Cover Design: JasonsCreative.com
Production and Composition: Eliot House Productions

This publication is designed to provide accurate and authoritative information in
regard to the subject matter covered. It is sold with the understanding that the publisher is not engaged in rendering legal, accounting, or other professional services.
If legal advice or other expert assistance is required, the services of a competent
professional person should be sought.

Library of Congress Cataloging-in-Publication Data
Levy, Scott.
    Tweet naked: a bare-all social media strategy for boosting your brand and
your business / Scott Levy.
    p.   cm.
    Includes index.
    ISBN-13: 978-1-59918-515-6 (pbk.)
    ISBN-10: 1-59918-515-6
    1. Social media. 2. Strategic planning. I. Title.
    HM742.L425 2014
    302.23'1—dc23   2013031172

Printed in the United States of America

18 17 16 15 14   10 9 8 7 6 5 4 3 2 1

Contents

Preface

Chapter 1

Chapter 2

Chapter 3

Building Your Brand 39

Chapter 4

Convergence Strategies and
Your Social Media Team 55

Chapter 5

Ways to Engage 75

Chapter 6

How to Build a Following 97

Chapter 7

Measuring and Monitoring Your Success 115

Chapter 8

Advanced Social Media Tips and Tricks 133

Author Note

Hey thanks for grabbing a copy of Tweet Naked, I think you'll love it and know it will help you take your Brand to the next level!

Before you go any further I want you to follow me on Twitter @FuelOnline Twitter.com/FuelOnline you'll understand why at the end of the book, but I vow to try and engage with you. I want to personally hear from you after you have read this book in order to thank you and get your feedback on it as well.

If you need anything at all please don't hesitate to contact us

916-915-3835, 533 Church Street, Suite 169, Nashville, TN 37219
Website: http://www.FuelOnline.co (NOT .com)

T http://www.Twitter.com/FuelOnline

F http://www.Facebook.com/FuelInternetMarketing

L http://www.Linkedin.com/in/FuelOnline

Foundations

was always what you would call a tinkerer. As a child, I would get a present and immediately want to know how it worked. So whenever I got a toy, or some type of gadget, I would take it apart to see what was inside. My parents were impressed when they saw how I put some of the gadgets back together after close examination of all of the parts. In fact, on occasion, I could even improve upon how the toy or gadget worked. Of course there were also those days when I was unable to reassemble the parts in front of me, and they were not at all amused, and I did get in a lot of trouble at times. From rewiring toys to telephones and building alarm systems, is who I was as a kid, and remains who I am today—someone interested in what makes things tick and how I can make them better.

Curiosity Spawns a Passion for Technology

This innate curiosity about how things worked would stay with me from those early years forward and with each new technological breakthrough. I remember when my family picked up our first home computer in the early 1980s. I was determined to see how this new and seemingly impossible machine worked. Unlike today, where it's common to find homes with several desktops, laptops, and tablets, the family computer at that time was a big deal, much as the TV set must have been three decades earlier. Computers were expensive items, so when my parents saw me approaching with my screwdriver, of course they were ready to have coronaries! I convinced them that I knew what I was doing and that if I looked inside, I could put it back together. It was also fortunate for me that I actually figured out how to do so.

It didn't take me long to figure out how computers worked. Because such skills were not yet being taught in the schools, I taught myself, mostly through trial and error. Computers and their capabilities—from both the hardware and software side—fascinated me. The possibilities seemed endless. I still remember watching the movie *Weird Science* in the mid-1980s and thinking that someday I, too, was going to create my own perfect woman as Anthony Michael Hall and Ilan Mitchell-Smith did when they attempted to create Lisa, played by the gorgeous Kelly LeBrock, in the film.

As I got older, one of my first computer activities was running a bulletin board service (BBS), which was a means of posting messages, meeting people, playing games, and building a community. At that time, we had an IBM 8066 as my dad's computer, and I got an IBM PC Jr., which was a lower-end "introductory" computer. It was nothing fancy but served my purposes for playing, exploring, programming in BASIC, and running bulletin boards. I still remember my WWIV board and the door games I had on it. Many people, me included, now consider these old bulletin boards as the precursor to the World Wide Web.

Of course it was painfully slow. I was using a 1,200-baud connection, so if I wanted to download something, such as a low-quality photo, it would take hours. I could literally hit the download button, have dinner, take a nap, and then, *presto*, three hours later the poor-quality photo would appear. Okay, it wasn't magic, but it was the best we had at the time.

By the start of the 1990s, the internet was just beginning to emerge. It had been used by the army, and then by some companies, but once the internet went public, everyone who was active in those early days of computer programming knew that this was going to be BIG. We knew it was just the beginning and could only imagine what our computer pages would look like a few years down the road.

Getting in on the Action

From the start, I was already speculating, and I wanted a piece of the action. So I immersed myself in how the World Wide Web worked. Many people didn't understand the concept, but I learned quickly about web pages and decided to start buying domain names. These were where the bulletin boards of the future would be built, on what we know as websites. At the time, domain names cost about $100 each and you had to buy them for two years—a big sum of money back then and especially for someone in college. I purchased several domain names.

Yahoo! owned GeoCities, which was a free homepage community in the mid-1990s, and it was the big dog out there. It offered extremely limited space, less than what we would use today to post a Facebook profile, but it was still a place to put photos and information about yourself, your business, or anything else. The homepages were crude, sort of the caveman equivalent of what we see today, but those of us who were computer mavens were quite intrigued nonetheless. I still loved to study everything closely to figure out how it worked and possibly improve upon it, so I immersed myself in this new technology. Sure enough, after learning how GeoCities worked, I decided that I could do a better job. So, while still in college and working at a tech support job, I decided to create my own free homepage community from my small apartment and compete against Yahoo!. I figured: Why not? Even Yahoo! had to start somewhere.

By 1997, I started my own business offering free homepages. My first order of business was to offer more space than GeoCities. They offered two megabytes; I offered 35. In comparison, just one Facebook profile today is about 1,000 megabytes. But at the time, 35 was unprecedented and pretty darn impressive. Apparently people were excited about having more space to post their profiles and photos, so they came in droves. Users posted all kinds of information about themselves, their families, their friends, their businesses, and anything else they could think of. It was "grass roots," very generic and transparent because people had no real reason not to be themselves.

I focused on learning how to get my site to come up in the search engines of that time, such as Alta Vista, Excite, and Infoseek. I knew if I wanted to compete I needed visibility and traffic. I spent a huge amount of time working with the system, constantly trying to refine it. I copied content, removed content, hid content, and experimented in all sorts of ways, analyzing why certain text, keyword density, and placement affected search results. Competition emerged quickly, so to stay one step ahead, I kept trying new things. After all, I wasn't breaking any rules, because there were no rules yet to break.

The other thing I realized was there is more to having a homepage, or your own domain, than you might imagine. If you wanted others to see it and benefit from your website, you would need to have it ranked high on search engines so people would find you. So I started to explore how my users could get their pages to come up higher on the search engine rankings.

As was so often the case, while my friends were out partying, I found myself sitting at the computer trying to figure out the key to search-engine ranking. I tinkered with all sorts of techniques and tactics, and in time achieved my goal. In fact, I ended up outranking Yahoo! GeoCities for free homepages. As a result, my community grew very fast.

Of course, the folks at Yahoo! were not pleased, and they let me know it with emails and even phone calls; after all, it was being upstaged by a college kid working from his tiny apartment. But I was still not doing anything wrong, so I continued to tinker, manipulating the search algorithms.

All good things come to an end, and when the dotcom bubble burst at the end of the '90s, I sold my homepage project to the highest bidder and moved on.

I took my skills at search engine optimization (SEO) and became a consultant, helping scores of site owners move to higher rankings, and I've been doing so ever since. I became quite successful in the field primarily because I was, and still am, very passionate about what I do. I've always been very analytical, which leads to plenty of research and scientific experimentation. I grew my own business, starting a company and hiring the best help I could find along the way. While many people in the industry became comfortable with the practices they were using, I knew the industry would continue to change rapidly so we kept on researching and confirming our results every single month so we could stay one step ahead.

It was also during this time that an entirely new subculture of technology and the internet emerged: social media. As I see it, behind the advent of the internet, social media was the next most significant event in the modern age of technology. It lit the internet on fire, changing what was a marvelous research tool into an interactive, global, social communications tool that has turned into a cultural phenomenon. It has empowered people, changed how we get our news, and forced improved customer service and transparency as well.

Social Media: The Humble Beginnings

I guess you could say those old bulletin boards were indeed the forerunners of social media, and they soon gave way to websites like Hot or Not and Face the Jury, which were online locations in which people could meet, share profiles and photos, or email one another. Then in 2002 came another player called Friendster, with the same basic meeting and dating approach. It was followed a year later by MySpace.

Founded by two employees of the international marketing company eUniverse (which became Intermix Media), MySpace took off very quickly. Being an early adopter, I joined MySpace early on. However, I was skeptical about this new platform from the start. My problem with MySpace was that they gave people too much freedom to do as they wanted on their pages. While this later resulted in all sorts of security issues, my concern from a technical point of view was that a page would take three and a half minutes to load with full sparkly, glittery, animated images, music playing, and a background that made everything unreadable. Sure, there were plenty of exciting bells and whistles that we discovered in the early days of the internet, but they were slowing down the interactive process that was emerging as (what we now call) social media. The longer you had to wait for all of this "stuff" to appear on your screen, the less exciting it became. MySpace pages were loaded with all sorts of clutter, so much so that it was hard to navigate and difficult to find what you were looking for.

Facebook, which began as a college-based membership site for Ivy Leaguers back in 2004, took off. The difference was that Facebook was very clean, very simple, and very easy to navigate. It did not feature animated things, all sorts of backgrounds and spam, but instead loaded pages quickly. Not unlike Google, which offered a clean and quick means of searching the web, Facebook made the user experience that much better.

From Facebook forward, a few unique social media sites have taken off, while many others have tried. Twitter, LinkedIn, and Pinterest, for example, each offer the user something slightly different from the other, and as a result, have thrived. Meanwhile, I stepped back from being an early adopter simply because I soon realized that there were too many social media sites appearing (and disappearing) and that they could not all compete.

That's the short version of my story—a kid who loved tinkering and turned pro—which brings me to why I'm writing this book. The book comes about mostly because I'm completely and genuinely passionate about what I do. I enjoy helping people generate success through their websites and through social media. It's rewarding to see my years of exploration and technical analysis paying off.

Social media has changed the we way we live and how information is distributed, and it's here to stay. It has crossed over from meeting and dating websites to a genuine form of networking and brand building as never before seen. Unlike TV and radio commercials, it is interactive, allowing the user to build relationships, and connections, which are so crucial to any type of business. If used correctly, social media can drive once-unimaginable numbers of followers to your brand, and do it in a way that is cost effective and can result in more business. But, as is the case with any medium, you need to know how to use it correctly. It can also be your worst nightmare if you put yourself and your brand out there in a manner that is inappropriate, offputting, and/or reckless.

Many young, well-meaning "social media experts" are popping up all over with six months of experience (or fake years). This worries me because when a company puts their trust in you, and possibly their entire marketing budget, the amount of damage you can do by not being good at what you do, not understanding enterprise-level requirements, is unthinkable. I've seen companies give every last penny to so-called SEO or social media experts only to be disappointed, have their reputations ruined, and even in terrible situations go out of business. Choose wisely, and do your due diligence.

I have followed the internet's development since it became public and have watched social media grow from its infancy to its current state of maturity, and I keep a close watch as it is still growing by leaps and bounds. I don't profess to know it all, but I've learned a lot in this business by studying it and using it, while always experimenting and running all sorts of tests. We consider not only SEO a science, but social media as well. There is so much that goes into what works, what doesn't, and why. Yes, I'm one of those people who could talk computer technology for hours and hours and never get tired of it. If I didn't love what I do, wasn't passionate about it, and didn't think we were one of the best companies out there at it, then I'd stop doing it and start doing something else (and I honestly would).

Chapter 1

What Is Social Media?

Social media is as appropriately named as any invention since the automobile, which automatically made you mobile. First, the term uses the word "social," which in this case refers to the act of being social, or socializing. It is about interacting and engaging people, treating people with respect, liking people so they will like you back, and communicating "with" them, rather than "at" them. The second part of the term is "media," which refers to a means of mass communication such as a newspaper, magazine, radio station, TV network, or website.

In essence, "social media" means you are socializing, or being social over a means of mass communication, or a form of media. It's not at all unlike broadcasting on your own TV channel. Everything you put out there is an imprint or an image of who you are, what you stand for, and what you are trying to communicate. Your messages, through your postings, impact the people with whom you are sharing the media, which may be a few friends and family or a mass following of several hundred thousand people. It depends on whether your media network is akin to a local cable channel or HBO.

By participating in social media, you *become* a form of media. Your entire audience can see each and every one of your posts and comments. Your audience may take away something positive or may think it's garbage. You may move them and inspire them, or disappoint and bore them. You may become a media star or embarrass yourself and lose credibility. Regardless of the size and scope of your audience, your messages will draw reactions that can be positive or negative. And unlike prior forms of media, the internet—and social media in particular—allows for instant feedback, so your every action can prompt a reaction.

It's Like Going to a Party

The best analogy for the social media is that it is similar to attending a party. You need to present yourself in the best manner if you want to be popular, make new friends, or even find that "special" someone with whom to establish an intimate relationship, even in the short term.

When you arrive at a party, you will typically look around, perhaps pour yourself a drink, and then begin interacting with other people. You might see a "hot" girl or guy you would like to meet, or see someone you already know. Do you walk up to these people and start selling them a product? Do you tell them you have the latest in state-of-the-art turbomatic vacuum cleaners at the lowest prices and can get them a great deal? Do you ask them to invest in REITS? Do you ask them again and again to pay attention to you, or "follow you" (which is the social media equivalent of paying attention to you)? People would likely roll their eyes and walk away, thinking that you are totally obnoxious. We've all met that guy or woman at a party. In some cases the person simply goes on and on about themselves regardless of whether anyone is listening or not. And what about the person who is crass, loud, and cursing? Is this the person you want to be? Yes, we see all kind of characters at a party or even at our local café or Starbucks.

You do not want to be one of these people. In a social setting, you want to be polite and respectful, meet people, share interests, be entertaining, alluring, funny, and perhaps even inform them of something that they may find fascinating. You want to engage in conversations that are not only about yourself. You also want to listen, because conversations are interactive and not monologues. While there are few, if any, rules posted on the door that dictate the specific ways a person must act while they are in the café or at the party, common sense should prevail.

Twitter is a giant digital cafe. It is the same landscape with loose rules and no specific criteria. Some of us are smart, courteous, and know how to interact appropriately, hoping people think well of us and want to communicate more often. Others abuse the situation and don't generate positive attention.

It's up to you to act accordingly and appropriately. Social media is that party or café, only magnified on a local, state, national, and even international level.

Your Social Media Goals

In the few short years since it was introduced, Twitter has grown from being a new-fangled toy for early adopters into a vast media tool for sharing mundane daily activities, spreading gossip, or building a business or a brand, which is our focus. Yes, it is only one of several forms of social media, but the concepts that we talk about for Twitter also apply to Facebook, LinkedIn, YouTube, Pinterest, and other platforms across the social media spectrum.

For our purposes, we are discussing the ways in which you can utilize Twitter to build your business and your brand, whether that means introducing yourself as a brand-new startup or reinventing yourself as a successful business taking on new challenges and providing new products and/or services.

DETERMINING YOUR BUSINESS GOALS

Here are five questions to help establish your social media business goals.

1. Are you looking to establish yourself as a topic expert?

2. Are you looking to build brand awareness?

3. Are you looking to revitalize a struggling company or grow your already successful business?

4. Are you looking for talented people to join your business?

5. Are you hoping to rebound from negative publicity or a sales slump?

In each case, you'll want to build a following, but your approach will differ. For example, establishing yourself as an expert means that you will discuss aspects of your business that others may learn from, or provide unique tips so that your followers can find shortcuts to meeting their needs. If, however, you are trying to revitalize a struggling business, you'll want to remind your followers of your company's history and discuss what new ideas are bringing it back. Your social media goals should remain at the forefront of your strategy as you post, pin, or tweet.

Your Responsibility

There's a popular saying: "With great power comes great responsibility." This is very true in social media because you are empowered, and the greater your empowerment, the greater your responsibility.

What you get out of being part of the media will be a direct result of what you put into it. For business purposes, social media is about growing a large following, because sales and revenue are a numbers game. The more people who know who you are and what you do, the more likely you will attract customers. Gaining followers is how you get a cult following and brand champions—people who help spread the word about you and your business, like unpaid PR reps.

Your audience, and subsequently, your responsibility, grows based on how much you put into it. Sure, it's easy to amuse or entertain a dozen friends from your postings because they know you and get your sense of humor. But it's quite different to entertain, impress, inform, and engage a following of 150,000 people, most of whom don't know you at all. It's not so easy.

It is, however, very easy to become known at some level on social media, and be "out there" and seen by hundreds of thousands of people. It was only a decade ago that you needed a chart-topping record or a role in a major movie to land yourself in the public eye. Today, it merely takes a few moments to establish a Twitter account to get you there. Countless people go online, make an impression, and become short-term celebrities without doing much more than being a jackass in the public eye. When you take the initiative to have an online presence, you immediately gain celebrity. At first, it isn't much. You arrive and someone starts watching everything you do. Then a few dozen are watching. Eventually, hundreds and maybe even thousands are watching you, some with a vested interest, others as casual observers. For some reason everyone likes to watch. YouTube is the perfect example of how we have become a voyeuristic society. We are inherently curious beasts that love to observe the good, the bad, the beautiful, and the ugly.

The Tweets you compose, the photos you take, filter, and share, and the videos you upload all manifest themselves as part of your own media. The longer you spend online, the bigger media presence you'll have, the more influential you are likely to be . . . and the more open to ridicule and criticism you are likely to become. The more you update and post and integrate other platforms with your persona, the more of your life is on display. You and your Twitter, Facebook, LinkedIn, and other profiles are all extensions of one another and ultimately feed off each other.

Social media large and small can reach many people very quickly, so if you do not act responsibly, you can get caught with your pants down, so to speak. Look at former New York Congressman Anthony Weiner, who learned the hard way that putting photos of his anatomy on social media would come back to haunt him and derail his political career. Many others have likewise learned that lesson the hard way, including athletes who have found themselves apologizing for behaving poorly.

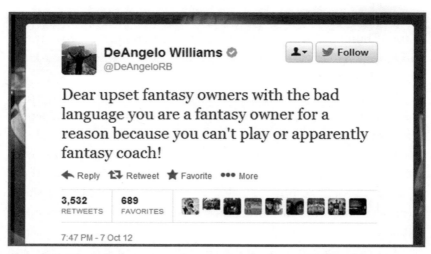

Figure 1–1 *The infamous tweet that prompted a barrage of hateful tweets directed at Williams*

In Figure 1-1, NFL running back DeAngelo Williams' tweet pokes at the very people who supported him as fans.

On the Other Hand . . .

Conversely, you can use your responsibility wisely. As a business owner or consultant, you might want to crowd-source information by asking your followers a question to get opinions, feedback, and input on a project. Perhaps you're doing market research and testing a logo, a slogan, or even a product. Maybe you want to poll people, start a petition against something unpopular in your industry, or discuss your customer service on a public stage to show everyone that you truly care about your buyers. A large following that respects you allows you to do all of these things, provided you act responsibly. This does mean you need to be prepared.

It is important to remember the very simple expression "think before you speak," or, in this case, tweet or post. From commercials to TV programs, everything is planned ahead of time, even on the supposedly "unscripted" reality shows. Likewise, magazine articles, newspaper stories, good web content, and successful blogs are read carefully and edited before being posted or printed. It's what most people do before posting their website or even their Facebook profile.

SOCIAL MEDIA ETIQUETTE

◆ *Don't say anything that you wouldn't say to your mother.*

◆ *Be nice!* This is a public stage and the spotlight is on you and your company. Being friendly and helpful goes a long way toward building your brand and reputation.

◆ *Don't be a showoff* and tout how great you are; a little humility does wonders when building a brand.

◆ *Don't sell or pitch.* Social media is for connecting, building relationships, networking, and creating brand awareness. Coming off as a snake-oil salesman is a huge turnoff.

◆ *Don't automate.* Social media is a two-way conversation, and automated posting is cold. Plus, you want to respond to all posts quickly—so unless someone is actively manning the battle station, your response times to your followers suffer.

◆ *Don't get angry.* If someone is complaining or being rude, reply professionally and never sink to their level.

◆ *Do care.* Take a minute out of your busy schedule to find out more about the lives of those who follow or like your pages. These are the people that can become your brand champions, so show them you care about who they are and what they do.

◆ *Give back!* If you've had great success via social media and people are sharing your brand, message, and products or services, then give back! A little thank-you discount, prize, or giveaway can go a long way and snowball, as recipients spread the word to their followers and friends. Social media users sharing your content and brand is absolutely invaluable, so show them you appreciate it and don't take it for granted.

Unfortunately, once people start interacting in social media, they often forget that the rules of good judgment still apply.

It is your responsibility to think like an editor and ask yourself, before you post:

- Do I really want my followers to read that?
- Will this increase my following?
- Am I providing something of value, whether it's newsworthy or a joke?
- Will it help my brand?
- Can it hurt me?
- Can it damage my business or brand's reputation?
- Am I insulting someone or a group of people?
- Am I spreading rumors, lies, or gossip that can damage someone's reputation?

It Can Make or Break Your Business

Many people simply appear on social media, making neither a positive nor negative impact. They blend into the crowd. While this is not necessarily a bad thing, it doesn't utilize the power of the media to its fullest advantage. Social media, in a few short years, has lifted brands from relative obscurity to significant popularity. How? By using the basic premise noted above: The more people following your brand or business, the more potential customers you have.

Some companies have done quite well in growing customer awareness and translating that into increased business. For example, the folks at Sharpie used their products to visually engage potential followers. They posted colorful, playful images on Pinterest and other visual platforms created by using Sharpie markers and pens. In an age when pens and marker sales are declining, according to *Ad Age*, Sharpie saw a 3 percent increase in sales thanks to the colorful social media campaign.

Richard McKay is director of McKay Flooring, founded by his father in Glasgow, Scotland, in 1973. McKay established himself as a flooring expert on Twitter and gained 50,000 followers by offering his flooring expertise to prospective customers. McKay also posts creative flooring ideas using company products on Pinterest and sent his followers to the company blog for more information, using cross-platform marketing and integration to increase business. McKay is now one of the UK's largest hardwood flooring companies.

Sole proprietors can also flourish. Ana White, an Alaska-based blogger, homemaker, and self-taught furniture maker created a website, ana-white.com, that empowers women to take on do-it-yourself home carpentry projects, from planning through the choice of finishes. White has amassed more than 50,000 Facebook fans, mostly women, by sharing easy ways of completing furniture projects. She invites her audience to share their own stories of building furniture or other items and has built an online community of people who not only share on her page, but among themselves, which grows White's following virally.

Of course, overzealous businesses looking to engage fans have also damaged their reputations by using social media badly, or through their own words, by posting before thinking.

Tweeting about news events means discussing them appropriately. Taking a tragic event and tweeting to gain a following in an effort to sell products does not sit well with potential customers. Just as no store owner would have a "9/11 one-day-only sale" (hopefully not), you need to be sensitive and politically correct in your tweets.

The initial backlash to tweets from The Gap and Kenneth Cole (Figures 1–2 and 1–3) came in the form of numerous tweets saying the posts were in poor taste. Both companies quickly issued apologies.

Cole himself responded with: "Re Egypt tweet: we weren't intending to make light of a serious situation. We understand the sensitivity of this historic moment —KC."

And two hours after that, Cole removed the tweet and apologized on Facebook.

Buyers have favorite big-name retailers and aren't so quick to let go, unless the company's egregious behavior hits home on a more direct level. For example, in 2009, two Domino's Pizza employees made a video for YouTube showing them violating food health and safety

Figure 1–2 *The Gap's post-Superstorm Sandy tweet*

Figure 1–3 *Another unacceptable combination: revolution and retail*

regulations, which quickly went viral. They caused far more damage to their company's brand than Cole or the Gap did with their own tweets. Because consumers eat Domino's products, the video hit home. The company made matters worse by not responding to it immediately, and as a result, in just a few days, Dominos lost 10 percent of its share value.

The damage that a thoughtless Tweet can cause a still-emerging brand can be devastating. Unlike the Gap, or Kenneth Cole, you don't

---

SOCIAL MEDIA DOS AND DON'TS

Do

◆ Be empathetic.

◆ Be tasteful.

◆ Engage with followers regularly—and quickly.

◆ Inspire with motivational saying and quotes.

◆ Educate by solving people's problems and by sharing your knowledge and expertise.

◆ Delight with entertaining comments or jokes.

◆ Respond in a timely manner, lest your followers feel ignored.

Don't

◆ Spam followers.

◆ Spread rumors or lies.

◆ Talk without listening. If you are putting yourself out there, expect responses, replies, praise, criticism, and other feedback. Pay attention to what others are saying to you.

◆ Lash out. Stop and think before you post or tweet, or have a checks and balances system so that anything going out is reviewed or scanned by at least a second pair of eyes.

◆ Be rude, crass, or vulgar.

◆ Fire someone without revoking access to your social media accounts.

◆ Exploit a tragedy or even bad news. It's offensive and in abysmally bad taste. And you're liable to lose even your most loyal followers.

---

have a massive following or longtime customer base, so you are more likely to watch customers walk away . . . wearing Kenneth Cole shoes.

Who Are You?

What will set you apart from the millions of other people using social media? Consider that nearly all media outlets today have formats and personalities in hopes of gaining an edge over their competitors. Some are geared to sports fans, some to news hounds, some to parents. They may cater to an age group, a religious affiliation, to political party members, or a specific industry, be it fashion or classic cars. With that in mind, you need to establish your online persona, your character, your format. Who do you most want to be the bulk of your followers? These are the people to whom you will want to direct your messages and build your following, which we'll tackle in Chapter 6.

I have a friend who only watches the Food Network. He loves to cook and knows exactly what he can expect, right down to the schedule of shows. And when he tweets or posts on Facebook, guess what he talks about? Food, restaurants, recipes, and cooking, and he's a damn good chef!

The same consistency can be found on SpikeTV, The Learning Channel, The History Channel, etc. Channels are the cable company's way of organizing their content so you can find the programs that match your interests. Other forms of media, from magazines to websites, also have formats, personalities, and character. This works very well for most of us who want to find what we like and find it quickly among so many options. There's a sense of comfort in knowing what to expect.

Should the channel or blogger stray from their format, viewership or readership drops. Just think of how disappointed you get when you turn to your favorite channel to watch the all-new episode of your favorite show, only to discover that they've changed their schedule.

I like to think of Twitter as the biggest cable network in the world. Instead of channels, there are user profiles. Instead of programs, there are tweets.

Like a TV channel, your audience will eventually come to expect certain things out of your "station." Routinely tweeting about personal financial security will quickly gain you an audience of people who want more insight into financial independence. Imagine their disappointment if you suddenly changed gears and only tweeted about luxury sports cars. Sure, you'd probably gain a new audience of car enthusiasts, but you're likely to lose the budget-minded individuals you had before.

Of course, change is not necessarily a bad thing, as long as what you transition into is consistent. If you are a sports channel one day, a weather channel the next, and a sports channel again the following day, you're going to have confused viewers who will eventually give up and find another channel to watch. Those we follow on Twitter are those from whom we've come to expect certain things. We follow them because what they do is consistent and meets our needs. In a world of niche markets, this is a good thing.

Be Ready to Wear Many Hats

Behind every TV show is an army of producers, directors, writers, and actors who work together to create the program that viewers tune into every week. Over time, TV shows gain audiences, refine their scripts, and develop a recognizable style and voice. If the show is good, we keep tuning in because we want to find out more about the characters and the story behind them. We love the drama, the humor, the escapism, and the human element. That human element is what we love about Twitter, Facebook, and the rest of social media as well. On Twitter accounts, it is fascinating to see the psychology behind the person revealed to us 140 characters at a time. It gives us something to relate to, something to interact with;it serves to remind us that on the other end of the fiber optic cables or radio waves is an actual human being who is sharing something with us. We especially like when emotions are bared and naked.

A team of writers that develops characters for a TV show is not unlike the Twitter user who is developing their audience and slowly developing an online persona one tweet at a time.

You have the job of that writer, creating your own character and your own lines. In addition, as station manager, you have to determine what your focus niche and "format" will be. And you are also the editor, deciding what goes "on air," so to speak, and what gets cut. This is where many social media users drop the ball, not realizing where to edit their content and what NOT to say. Millions of people every day realize one second after tweeting that maybe they should have edited their comment. Others catch on more slowly.

Social media is much more than a passing fad. Let's face it, we like communicating with other people from friends down the street to people on the other side of the globe. We like being able to express ourselves when we want, how we want, and draw attention to what we have to say and build our business or brand. This is true across all social media platforms.

Choose and Focus

When it comes to choosing which social media platforms you'll utilize, select those that offer the best potential for reaching your ideal audience and broadcast the type of media you've decided is best suited for your company. Most people and companies can't be amazing on every platform; that takes a huge amount of bandwidth and resources. Instead of having a sub-par representation in a lot of places, be awesome on a few of them. Then comes your strategy to decide what content you'll push out where. Some may be duplicated if it's truly important, but each site should get some of its own unique content as well. Depending on the site, you may provide your messages in photos, videos, short conversations, or status updates. In Chapter 4, we'll delve into building your social media strategy over multiple platforms.

But whatever platforms you use, the key to success is having the time to devote. Social media is made up of interactive tools, so what you put out there will generate responses. If you don't respond to your fans or followers, you'll be wasting your time and will lose those customers or clients.

So, Which Social Media Platforms Will You Embrace?

Some people like to be a part of everything going on; they have 100 movie channels and each new tech gadget that comes out. In the social media world, there are numerous platforms available. The problem is that we only have so much time to post, interact, and make our presence felt on any of these platforms. Like me, most businesspeople embrace a few of the major platforms, but have a favorite to which they devote more of their time and attention. For me that is Twitter. However, I also use Facebook, LinkedIn, and visit other platforms, but that's part of my job.

How do you decide which platforms are best for your needs? Here is a brief overview of the most significant platforms as they pertain to your business needs.

PINTEREST

Pinterest is billed as a content-sharing service that allows members to pin or post photos, videos, and other images to their pinboards.

An amazing newcomer to social media, Pinterest utilizes the fact that we are visual creatures by nature and features powerful, motivating images that convey ideas and concepts visually.

The site, which has a predominantly female audience, is ideal for businesses for which visual imagery is a main feature or selling point. If you focus on wedding planning, travel destinations, interior decorating, fashion or foods, you can say a great deal about your products and services through your stunning photos or videos. FAB.com features marvelous photos of interesting, unique products, some of which people have never seen before. If you are, like me, sitting behind a computer all day, you probably don't have great images to show that will benefit your brand.

In essence, Pinterest has a niche market and serves it very well. You can comment on people's boards, share imagery, and click onto the webpages from which the images came. You can also like what you see, or "pin it." Each board is linked to the pinner's profile page so people can see the person, business, or brand behind the photos or videos.

LinkedIn

LinkedIn is the consummate networking site. Even before the term "social media" became fashionable, we had social networking, and that clearly defines LinkedIn. It is a way of growing connections in the business world and utilizing them as necessary.

In many respects, it is like a massive online phone book or database where you can find a copyeditor, angel investor, insurance agent, marketing manager, or whomever you may be looking for. It is great for reaching out to people and getting into their Rolodex, so that when they need your services, there you are. It also includes groups and discussions where you can politely discuss your interests, show that you are transparent, solicit advice, ask questions, and answer questions, letting your expertise impress others. Service providers are more prevalent than manufacturers or retailers, because it's easier to talk about what you do or what your business does, and it's not a very visual medium.

One of the biggest problems on LinkedIn is that too many people misuse it as a social site and just chat or use it to sell and pitch, which is frowned upon or ignored. Like many others, I post links to my articles or blogs so people can read more about who I am and what I do.

YouTube

YouTube is a very powerful tool, visually driven and potentially very exciting. It has become synonymous with homemade or company-made videos. It is watched worldwide and people post videos with hopes of going viral.

The key to using YouTube effectively is to feature your product or service in an unforgettable way, and with millions of people now using YouTube, the bar is set very high. No one will watch a boring video.

One great example of how YouTube can take your product or service to the next level is from Blendtec, a company that makes state-of-the-art blenders and mixers. They thought it would make a statement if they would show the strength and power of their products with a series called "Will It Blend?" This included tossing anything from glow sticks to iPhones to speakers into the blenders to see if they would blend, and they did! And it was fun to watch.

Like Pinterest, you can use YouTube to capitalize on our innate love of visuals. It's a good idea to watch a number of YouTube videos and see which ones generated hundreds of thousands (or even millions) of hits. Videos that show people how to do something, demonstrate your product or service, or introduce a new or unusual (visual) product can help you benefit from YouTube.

TWITTER

Twitter is an ongoing conversation that, like text messaging, has become widely popular. Unlike Facebook and other social media platforms, where people can choose what to look at on your site, or respond later, Twitter is more immediate and "in the moment."

It is a marvelous tool for businesses that want to reach out to people now and expect—and are ready for—people to reply. If you have breaking news, updates, questions for your followers, or if you want opinions now,or even need to announce a recall, Twitter is the way to reach out to people. It's for the business that has things to say frequently and prefers to reach people directly. You want people to get to know you from your ongoing conversation and learn more about you and what you have to offer.

FACEBOOK

Facebook is an extraordinary platform that has impacted American culture. Heck, they even made a movie about the founder. It is one of the most powerful platforms in the world. Facebook's size alone is a positive for any business, because you can assume most people are on it.

Unlike Twitter, you can choose what to look at, whether it is a profile, photos, videos, etc., and what you want to share. This gives businesses and brands more opportunities to represent themselves in various ways. Facebook is about a long-term commitment and building relationships. It is for people who are in it for the long haul, although there is some immediacy as you can reply directly to people's comments or questions.

Almost any business can benefit from having a Facebook page. But, if left unattended, which is a common problem, you won't be leveraging it as the interactive tool it was meant to be. Remember, Facebook is all about sharing and interacting. Managing your Facebook page and responding to people who contact you can help you tell your story.

Facebook isn't about selling. Your goal in using Facebook for business is to let customers get to know the people behind the logo. You'll want to portray your business in a friendly, "sociable" manner, as a place where customers are treated well and "everybody knows your name." For example, photos should illustrate not just you at your desk, but your dog at a company event, or your staff all teaming up to work at Habitat for Humanity. It's not just about the fact that you like to recycle, but that your business culture includes recycling. If done correctly, your fans become loyal followers and Facebook can be a very significant lead generator.

GOOGLE+

Google+ is similar to Facebook, with some of the qualities of the other platforms. Personally, I am not a big fan. Google+ arrived late to the party and seems to have been created for the sake of having a social media platform. You automatically become a member when you sign up for a gmail or a YouTube account.

While each of the other five platforms discussed here have a distinct character and are the best at what they do, Google+ doesn't have its own distinction. People can post to their "circles," which is like "friends" on Facebook. Nonetheless, Google+ is another means of reaching out to a large audience in a transparent manner with information about yourself, your business, and/or your brand. Most businesses can benefit from the exposure and potential leads.

It's hard to be on all platforms, so choose the three that best meet your needs and monitor—or hire someone to monitor—them closely. Social media only works if you stay involved. However, to do this well and make it worthwhile, you need to understand that your social media presence is a form of media, which means you need to wear the various hats, be consistent, understand your responsibilities, and, as we'll discuss in the next chapter, be transparent.

Transparency and Authenticity

Transparency and authenticity are more than just "buzz words" in business today. They are what a rapidly growing number of consumers expect from the companies with which they do business. Quite frankly, people are sick and tired of big corporate monsters being untouchable and indifferent or aloof. The days of these reclusive, faceless companies are disappearing. People want accurate, timely information. They want full disclosure. They want honesty in business and expect corporations of all sizes to provide transparency and authenticity. They also want to know the human beings behind the website, the logo, the commercials, and the print ads. And it's not only in business or corporate America that transparency is in demand by the public. It is obviously significant in the political arena, and in our schools where we want to know who is educating our children and what is being done to keep our children safe. It is in law enforcement and in government agencies. Nonprofit groups are also held accountable as well as community groups and even neighborhood associations.

In fact, not long ago, Google released the number of requests by the FBI for people's online activity. It illustrated how a major social media platform could take the lead in how to be transparent.

Of course, companies will still hold closed-door meetings and keep their trade secrets to themselves—all perfectly legal. After all, they need to maintain a competitive edge. But honesty and openness with customers is the new "sexy" when it comes to doing business.

Today, your personal brand, or business, needs to exhibit the same transparency when it comes to social media. As I see it, transparency and authenticity are the new reality TV. People are bored and tired of the same old scripted messages repeated again and again. They watch reality TV, even if it is not completely authentic, because they see real people with their own successes and their failures, as well as their shortcomings and gifts. It's real, and people form relationships and draw connections with characters.

You are now creating a character in social media that is honest and based on who you really are.

Transparency applies to everything from who you are to what you stand for, and all of that is important for an industry expert, a small business owner, or a Fortune 500 executive. No matter who you are, people want you to be open, honest, and straightforward. You're like the chef at a fine restaurant who comes out of the kitchen and shakes the customer's hands and talks about preparing the food; the athlete who drops the cliché answers and tells it like it is; the executive who fields questions from the podium and gives honest answers about the products, the merger, or the news of the day. You're the expert who says the product, the service, the test site, or the film is not yet ready for the public, and here's why. You are someone who believes in being open, honest, and transparent—within the boundaries of common sense and good taste, of course.

Be Yourself

Oscar Wilde once said, "Be yourself; everyone else is already taken." And that brings us to the topic of your own personal transparency, which means being open, sincere, and, in essence, yourself. Quite honestly, the easiest character to create and portray should be "you," right? Comedian Lewis Black might dispute that, as he does in a comedy routine in which he talks about a TV network executive who once wanted to do a show based on his life, but didn't want to play himself in the show. Black was baffled about someone wanting to replace himself to play himself! Odd as that sounds, most of us are well versed enough to play ourselves, at least on the internet. We have years of experience, and we know what we like, dislike, and care about. We know our strengths, our weaknesses, our goals, and even our favorite foods!

Yet many people are still not comfortable being themselves. Insecurity and years of putting up walls to protect ourselves have left many of us feeling awkward and uncomfortable about revealing who we really are. In fact, a recent study by Hubspot, a social media monitoring service, found that upwards of 40 percent of "active" Twitter users

---

YOU KNOW YOU HAVE CHARACTER WHEN . . .

You exhibit:

- ◆ Honesty and integrity
- ◆ Likes, dislikes, interests, passions, etc.
- ◆ Goals, desires, and what you want to achieve
- ◆ Expertise
- ◆ Vulnerability and weaknesses, because nobody is perfect

It is important for you to expose your human, vulnerable side (with some limits and cautions; see "Doing It Wrong: Transparency Can Hurt You" on page 34) in order to gain the trust of your audience.

---

never actually tweet. One reason is that they aren't comfortable being themselves, being naked online, or even semi-naked. Fret not—we were all there at one point. Many of us sat there looking at other people's tweets, thinking, "I don't know what to say. Who will be interested in me or my brand anyway?"

So how do you—Character A—present yourself so you can build an audience and engage Characters B, C, D, etc.? What will you tweet to get an audience's attention? What will make them follow you? How will your online character engage someone else? By creating a character based on who you are, what you do, and what you are passionate about.

How to Be Transparent

For a business, there is much more to transparency than providing your annual report or putting the ingredients on your packaging. People want to connect; they don't want that automated phone system, but the human being instead. It's about being engaging, sharing passions, and talking about your brand as it relates to real people.

There are many ways in which to exhibit transparency.

Share Your Successes

Share your successes, such as closing a big deal, winning an award, or getting a major accolade, by showing your humility and enthusiasm, not by tooting your own horn or bragging. Showing that it really means something to you to win an award is a very honest reaction. People get excited when they win something, and it is human to share it (see Figure 2–1 on page 23).

Street Roots, publishers of a biweekly street newspaper in Portland, Oregon, sold by homeless vendors, shared its latest initiative on its Facebook page. Positive initiatives, not unlike winning an award in your community, should be shared. They let followers and fans know you are proud of your achievements while also reminding them of your brand (see Figure 2–2, page 23).

Figure 2–1 *Education at Work, a Cincinnati, Ohio, nonprofit that provides jobs and training to college students, announces a new partnership with Vantiv Inc., a payment-processing service, via Google+.*

Figure 2–2 *Sharing a positive initiative.*

Share Your Passions

Talk about the community food drive you ran, the Little League team you sponsor, or the greener mode of transportation people are using to get to and from the office. New Belgium Brewery in Colorado is gung-ho about having their employees bicycle to work every day to keep the air quality just a little cleaner—and gives them free bikes for doing so. They love talking about making the world a little greener through sustainable practices, from recycling to using rainwater in their brewery. Perhaps you and your employees get your hands dirty working for Habitat for Humanity or in some other community effort. Share this with people.

Many businesses today are involved in nonbusiness activities. Companies of all sizes stepped up to provide relief after Superstorm Sandy rocked the Northeast in October 2012, with devastating floods causing billions of dollars of damages. Companies provided volunteers and raised money. Talking about the role your business played in relieving the effects of such a tragedy is more than just good PR; it shows a genuine concern for others.

Let people know about your interests and hobbies as well. Just like in the real world, it's a great way to start a conversation—and to let people know the person behind the brand. I let people know what music I like to listen to, what I get excited about, the football team I root for (the Tampa Bay Buccaneers). I try to build a relationship with my audience by trying to be authentic and mixing who I am with what I know about my business.

People gravitate to those with whom they share interests. If, for example, you are looking for a lawyer, are you more likely to choose one who shares that she is a dog or cat lover or is into sailing, or one who only talks legalese?

Talk About Your Corporate Culture

This is a great way to win your followers' trust. They learn how your company conducts business and how you treat your employees. It is a way of reminding followers of the age-old saying "We do business with people we like and trust." How can you like people and trust them if you don't know who they are or what they stand for?

Let potential followers and customers see the human side of business and appreciate the candor. Talk about the funny things that happen in the office such as the Super Bowl bet the CEO lost to an office temp. Discuss group outings or activities such as how the company softball team got clobbered, or how the sales department managed to capsize their canoe on the company fishing trip. Do you have casual days? Do you bring your kids to work on occasion? Do you have free medical screenings? What is it like working in your business? Even a one-person operation has stories to tell about their work atmosphere that are very real and engaging.

Let People Know You Aren't Perfect

Transparency is not all about your successes. From recalls of anything from aspirin to automobiles, to airlines losing luggage, things go wrong in every industry. Those companies that try to hide it or act like it didn't happen are the ones that lose customers in a major way once the truth gets out . . . and it almost always does.

Being honest, transparent, humble, and admitting you screwed up is what transparency is also about. It's in vogue today to step up and acknowledge that changing the age-old formula in your popular soft drink was a big mistake or that the newer, faster processor was a dud. Being honest and authentic means talking about your failures and showing humility when you ship something to the wrong place, get called out for a code violation, or find yourself in the news for a billboard others found offensive.

Apologizing and talking about your errors makes people relate to you and creates empathy. Some companies have figured out that transparency means telling it like it is. For example, Jet Blue and Virgin Air respond to customer complaints, make jokes about their errors, and correct mistakes in public to show people that they are transparent and working to make their businesses better.

JET BLUE'S SOCIAL MEDIA STORY

Jet Blue adopted social media early on to connect and communicate with customers, with founder and CEO David Deeleman using YouTube as early as 2007 to apologize for the cancellation of 1,200 flights when an ice storm unexpectedly hit the New York metropolitan area and the company was unprepared to manage the crisis.

The company then adopted blogging, Twitter, and YouTube as its main social channels for communication and issuing *mea culpas*.

On Feb. 14, 2011, a Jet Blue plane sat on the tarmac of a snowy Connecticut runway for more than seven hours. Passengers had no access to food, water, or working bathroom facilities, nor were they offered an explanation as to why they were waiting for such a long time before taking off. At least one angry passenger tweeted from the plane during the entire ordeal, which, including flight time, lasted 11½ hours. Jet Blue's apologetic response to customers and the public again came in the form of a personal statement of responsibility, this time by the company's COO, posted to YouTube and to the company blog.

The company routinely responds individually to angry customers via Twitter and has continued to offer communication via social channels. Utilizing humor and keeping their customers informed, Jet Blue has successfully leveraged social media to keep customers happy, as shown in Figure 2–3.

Jet Blue has also engaged followers in conversations about mutual topics of interest. Flier Louie Baur, for example, tweeted back and forth with Jet Blue about their mutual love of ninjas, building a bond between the company and the client. Such personal bonds can create tremendous brand loyalty.

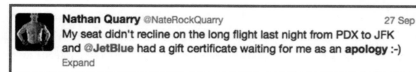

Nathan Quarry @NateRockQuarry   27 Sep
My seat didn't recline on the long flight last night from PDX to JFK and @JetBlue had a gift certificate waiting for me as an **apology** :-)
Expand

Figure 2–3 *Social Media evidence that Jet Blue recovered from previous bad PR events through its clever and consistent use of social media.*

THE KITCHENAID® DEBACLE

During the 2012 election debates, a member of the social media team at KitchenAid "accidentally" tweeted a disparaging remark about President Barack Obama's grandmother, who had passed away just a few days earlier.

KitchenAid
@KitchenAidUSA

Obamas gma even knew it was going 2 b bad! 'She died 3 days b4 he became president'. #nbcpolitics

Figure 2–4 *The tweet that set off a backlash of negative responses*

The numerous responses to KitchenAid's inappropriate tweet included comments about not registering for KitchenAid products; throwing out those products; telling KitchenAid to stick to mixers and stay out of politics; and the basic reminders that insensitive, inappropriate jokes do not go over well with current, or potential, customers.

KitchenAid responded quickly, taking full responsibility for their social media team's poor and careless action. Cynthia Soledad, head of the KitchenAid brand, tweeted that that they would "personally like to apologize to President Barack Obama, his family, and everyone on Twitter for the offensive tweet sent earlier." She also sent an email to various online media sites, including Mashable and The Huffington Post, expressing regret and apologizing for the incident (see Figure 2–5, page 28).

In contrast, other companies make it impossible to reach anyone when something goes wrong or a customer is in need of assistance. As

> During the debate last night, a member of our Twitter team mistakenly posted an offensive tweet from the KitchenAid handle instead of a personal handle. The tasteless joke in no way represents our values at KitchenAid, and that person won't be tweeting for us anymore. That said, I lead the KitchenAid brand, and I take responsibility for the whole team. I am deeply sorry to President Obama, his family, and the Twitter community for this careless error. Thanks for hearing me out. –Cynthia Soledad, senior director, KitchenAid

Figure 2–5 *KitchenAid's apology.*

a result, they generate numerous negative postings all over social media and on websites, which, in time, can significantly hurt sales.

The Art of Vulnerability

Being vulnerable is more than just saying, "Oops, we screwed up." It's opening up a little about you, letting us know that behind the smoke and mirrors is the real Wizard of Oz and he's just an ordinary guy, like the rest of us.

People fear vulnerability because they are scared that showing any signs of weakness will spoil their mystique or their competitive edge. And yet, today, being naked and vulnerable is becoming a strength. It can break down the wall between you, your brand, your logo, and your followers. BUT you need to do so correctly.

Vulnerability is not about telling dark secrets, but about sharing the human struggles and concerns of life. Let people know what you are looking to learn more about or discuss the challenges you may have overcome or are hoping to overcome in the future. Acknowledge that you are baffled by some of the latest technology or that you are not yet where you'd like to be at the gym. If you are successful in your field, talk about how your business emerged from your garage, your brother-in-law's basement, or some other humble starting point. Talk about the early struggles, within reason, of course. People can relate to building something from nothing, and especially to the trial and error process.

Look for others who are vulnerable and let them know that you've been there and done that. "Like" the post on Facebook or LinkedIn about not knowing how to use your iPhone when you first got it or respond to the tweet from someone who doesn't understand what hashtags are or how to use them.

But even better than simple, everyday vulnerabilities are those that pertain directly to what it is that you do. If you monitor hashtags and keywords related to your expertise, then you have a real opportunity to be the knight in shining armor or Wonder Woman to the rescue. Demonstrating your knowledge and willingness to be helpful can go a long way in winning over fans and brand champions.

Of course, vulnerability can only go so far. There's a fine line between being vulnerable and letting the horses out of the barn. Go slowly, and like a classic stripper, get naked a little at a time. Bottom line is vulnerability equals being real and authentic.

FIVE WAYS TO TALK BUSINESS WITHOUT BEING PUSHY OR PITCHY

1. *Ask general questions.* Asking questions opens the door to learning more about the other person. It's an old sales technique, but is effective because the more you learn, the easier it is to determine how your product or service can (or can't) help them.

2. *Solve problems.* You build tremendous credibility if you, as an expert, can simply help people solve a problem related to your product or services.

3. *Discuss mutual (brand-related) interests.* If you are in the food industry, talk restaurants or recipes; if you are a contractor, talk about homes or offices. The more you connect on a general basis, the easier it will be to discuss what you do.

4. *Use anecdotes and stories.* If you have an entertaining anecdote that relates to your business or industry, by all means, share it to draw people in.

5. *Show photos of things you love.* If they also like what they see, they may come to you to find out how to achieve such a beautiful garden or where to get such a great power tool.

Include Your Expertise

Of course, you are still an expert, a personal brand and/or representing a company, so you do need to talk about what you know and impart some information along the way. You need to play a dual role, being personable and honest while also talking shop. But don't get overeager when it comes to talking business. Social media users can spot a sales pitch before you finish your tweet or your post. And like the guy trying to sell you real estate investments at a party or social gathering, you'll be shunned quickly.

Subtlety is the name of the game when it comes to talking business in social media. Your objective is to engage others in conversations about your area of strength and show that you know what you are talking about. Showing knowledge and expertise is how they come to respect you rather than saying "buy this product," or "use my service." The trick is getting them to want to use your services or champion your brand without asking.

Transparent Profiles

If you really want to let people know a little more about you, it's very important, on all platforms, to carefully and honestly fill out your profile.

Don't hide behind a title, a business name, or a user name, but instead let potential followers know who you really are. You can always link to your business website if they want to know more about the business, but the profile is about you.

On Twitter, your bio must be brief, so you need to edit carefully. On other platforms you have more room to expand, but don't overdo it. Be brief and to the point about who you are and what you do professionally. Then include a little personal information, such as father of three, married, dog lover, Little League coach, jazz vocalist, or skiing enthusiast. You want to go beyond your job and title so that people see your human side. It's also a good idea to include your location. This way people not only have an idea of your whereabouts but it's a good starting point for connecting. Someone looking at your profile may have visited your region recently, may know someone living there, or it may be someplace they've always wanted to visit.

Your photo is important, too. It should be a clear headshot with a smile. Some people try to be too clever and have an offbeat photo that

---

YOUR PROFILE PICTURE

As you spend more time on social media platforms, you are bound to see many "don'ts" when it comes to profile photos. Here are 10 of my favorites:

1. Don't use a prom photo or anything that resembles one.

2. Don't use an old photo; it's not a dating website. If your profile says that you graduated college in 1989 and your picture makes you look like you're still 22 years old, people will become suspicious.

3. Don't use an obvious vacation photo. That Hawaiian shirt or hula skirt may be well received by friends and family on your personal Facebook page, but not for building a following when it comes to business.

4. Don't use a group photo. It's a profile picture, not a police lineup.

5. Photos of your pet can work, but at least be in the photo with them. Don't pose Fluffy the iguana by himself.

6. Don't go for artsy or "cute." One guy's profile photo was of a teddy bear in a military uniform. Not sure what the message was, but it certainly wasn't transparency.

7. Don't use ANY photo taken in the bedroom.

8. Don't use a photo from the last formal occasion you attended. This is about being who you are on a day-to-day basis, so unless you're a maitre d', wearing a tuxedo looks odd.

9. Don't do the "looking over the shoulder" pose.

10. Don't wear clothes that were last fashionable before social media existed.

---

doesn't fairly represent who they are. One gentleman on LinkedIn has a photo of himself wearing a top hat and glancing over his shoulder. He looks more like a gangster from an old movie than someone you would want to engage with.

It's a Two-Way Street

One of the biggest drawbacks of traditional media is that in most instances, you cannot respond. It's a one-way street with the producers, writers, and editors giving you their programming, their articles, and their messages. Businesses show you a commercial or the print ad or billboard, and your only way to respond is to yell at the TV set at a product you hate.

Social media is a two-way street in which customers, potential customers, fans, and critics can all interact with you. Remember, you are a form of media. Social media lets people talk to you and respond to whatever you put out there. It also lets you respond by telling them what you are doing to improve your product or service so they will believe in you and trust you.

With just a few keystrokes you can acknowledge that you screwed up the customer's order and send him a free case of the product. You can explain company decisions and thinking behind the new recipes, or the construction of the latest software program or power mower. You can even ask for feedback on your ideas in advance. Rather than holding elaborate focus groups, you can use social media to say, "We're thinking of selling organic tomato sauce, what do you guys think about that?" You can get some amazing feedback. Rather than just making a business decision, your customers can now be part of the conversation and part of the decision. And let's face it, when people are involved in the process, they are far more interested in the results.

For example, Sam Adams does crowdsourcing via social media to create new beers. "The Crowd Craft Project" allowed Sam Adams' consumers to give feedback on the company's latest offering, commenting on a number of categories to describe the beer, such as color and body. The most popular categories as selected by Facebook

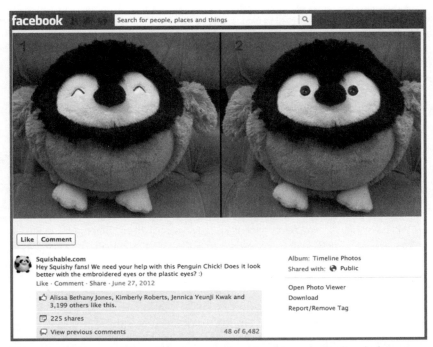

Figure 2–6 *Using social media to get product development feedback direct from customers.*

fans were then used by the company's brewers to develop the new beer, which débuted in March 2013 during the annual South by Southwest festival in Austin, Texas. It was then served in a number of Austin bars and at the company's brewery before being released more broadly.

In Figure 2-6, Squishable.com asked Facebook fans which stuffed animal design they should run with.

For those wondering and staying up nights waiting for the results, Penguin Chick No. 1, on the left, won out—and sold out.

Retweeting customer tweets is also a great idea. This way, you can post some of the many tweets your business gets—both positive and negative. Tweeting only accolades and testimonials that proclaim how wonderful your product or service is can begin to sound a bit too scripted. Consumers today are savvy and they know that nothing is 100 percent terrific. By being honest and tweeting naked about both

---

HOW TO RETWEET A NEGATIVE RESPONSE

UberTroll: Hey @uberorganicsauce Gotta say I tried your new organic sauce and it sucked.

UberOrganicSauce: Thanks for reaching out to us @UberTroll We'd love to know what you didn't like about it or how we can make it even better for you.

UberOrganicSauce: @UberTroll we'd be happy to send you a discount coupon if you'd like to try it again or one of our other products.

While you may or may never appease a truly dissatisfied customer, making the effort to do so illustrates your company's desire to satisfy even your harshest critics.

---

the positive and negative comments, you show people that you are not intimidated by negative feedback and that you are acknowledging, and responding to, them in an honest manner. By accentuating the positives but acknowledging the negatives and being upfront and honest, you will generate far more respect from your followers.

Doing It Wrong: Transparency Can Hurt You

Yes, you want to be open and honest, but there are limits. Publicly bashing someone, taking strong stands on highly controversial issues that are unrelated to your business—such as politics or religion, or dropping f-bombs or other inappropriate words or phrases—is not what transparency is really about and can hurt you. You're not trying to shock people or offend them in hopes of getting a rise out of them. Instead, you are trying to build a relationship as adults. If you wouldn't say something around your mother, then don't say it in social media.

Transparency does not mean you can post or tweet anything about anyone. You need to be very cautious about infringing on the rights of other people as well as being aware of potential copyright violations—say, by posting photos of other people. YouTube is constantly removing sports highlights that someone posts from a source such as ESPN without having permission to do so.

Every day, Twitter receives numerous allegations and complaints of unauthorized use of a copyrighted images or tweets containing links to allegedly infringing materials. While they cannot police all of these possible infringements, they do their best, as does YouTube, Facebook, and other social media platforms, to catch offenders. Twitter has trademark policies available if you aren't sure about the rights to use a photo, link, or logo.

You can state the truth about what other people are doing, but you must make sure you are accurate and then think about potential fallout. Tackling hot issues can be tricky, because you may win over loyal followers, but also lose objectors. Before you take on a topical issue, determine whether you believe you have more to gain than lose.

Transparency also does not mean providing an ongoing account of your every activity during the day. Friends may do this on Facebook, but for brand building, you need to provide enough honesty without becoming tedious and self-absorbed. If you put honest, real messages out there, and let people absorb them, you can continue to build your brand. If you overdo it, you can lose them due to information overload. We'll return to this idea later.

Another important aspect of the media is accuracy. You must consider the accuracy of your statements. Yes, you can always apologize for an error if you say something that is incorrect, not unlike when a newspaper prints a retraction. But if errors and inaccurate information become commonplace, you can seriously damage your brand's or business's reputation. With that in mind, take a moment and look up the information before you post or tweet something.

Consistency Counts

Let's face it, if someone says one thing one day and something completely different the next, unless they are a politician, you will be confused and taken aback. Consistency is important in social media, especially when it comes to how you present yourself or taking a stand on something important. That's why it is important to be honest. If you say you are a Buffalo Bills fan one month and then decide you're a Dolphins fan the next, chances are you won't lose too many followers, outside of Buffalo, that is. But if you advocate one position on Twitter but take a very different stance on Facebook, people will catch on. Social media followers typically interact with one another on other platforms.

All of this goes back to being honest about what you do, how your business operates, and what you stand for, lest you lose credibility, which will be extremely hard to rebuild. For example, if Piers Morgan suddenly became a hard-edged news reporter, or Chef Ramsey—who loves to scream and shout—became a quiet, nice guy, we'd be a bit taken aback by their new characters. Paul Rubens took a major hit in popularity to his beloved children's character, Pee-Wee Herman, when he was found pleasuring himself in an adult movie theater. It took Rubens quite a while to make a comeback. There are many examples of people in the public eye whose lack of consistency cost them fans and followers. While most are able to regain their following's trust, if inconsistency in the character you project becomes a regular occurrence, you may not win people back.

Negativity and Positivity

There are two ways to approach social media. You can see the "virtual glass" as being half empty or half full. Plenty of people enjoy complaining or trashing others on social media platforms, especially on Twitter. For me, this doesn't work. In fact, negativity is a pet peeve of mine. I don't think it is an attractive quality that draws people to you.

Sure, we all agreed that we despised Bin Laden and that the economy is struggling; the news will tell us that and other negative stories. However, on social media you have the opportunity to empower, inspire, and motivate people. I have fans and followers who will ask me advice on a job interview and I'll give them positive reinforcement. I also put up motivational quotes or something amusing and people will thank me for brightening their day. Isn't it more likely that when someone wants to do business with a company, they will choose the brand that makes them feel good and inspired? People who are constantly voicing complaints, knocking or trashing something, or putting up negative comments attract less people. This is true almost anywhere you go. Do you like spending more time with someone who constantly complains, or with someone who makes you smile and is inspiring or motivating? A positive, uplifting approach can almost always win more friends and followers than being a downer. Plus, it makes you feel good when people respond to your comments, suggestions, and jokes.

In the end, transparency and authenticity will be your most effective tools when it comes to engaging people. They will know you better, trust you most, and when it comes to doing business will think of you and your brand before they think of your competitors.

Chapter 3

Building Your Brand

One of the most critical aspects of any business is its brand. Your brand defines your business to the world and differentiates it from your competitors. It is also your brand that people remember and hopefully champion. But a brand is more than just a logo or a slogan. Your brand tells both current and potential customers what they can expect from your business. It is the personality and the character of the business and the promise to provide the best service and/or products to your customers. It's all the elements that make you the awesome company that you are.

While many companies wrestle with how to brand themselves, the most successful source of brand creation is, very simply, passion. I tell new entrepreneurs that before they spend money, invest in their businesses, or hire anyone, they need to have a passion for what they do, what they make, or what services they offer.

The New Brand Building: Sharing Enthusiasm and Creating Likability

For years, companies talked at you, telling you what to buy and giving you their reasons why you needed their products. Brands were disguised behind logos, faceless companies, and clever catch phrases. Customers were simply recipients of the messages, but were not actively involved. It was the company providing you with what they wanted to share. Today, that has turned around nearly 360 degrees, thanks largely to social media. Brands can be built and marketed by your followers, by those who love what you do, what you say, what you stand for, what you sell, and how you treat your customers.

Word-of-mouth is the biggest marketing tool that you could possibly ask for (and one of the cheapest). Tweets, posts, emails, texts, and other means of sharing comprise how numerous brands evolve today and remain leaders in their industries. My own business, Fuel Online (http://www.FuelOnline.co), which specializes in high-level SEO and social media management, is a perfect example. All of our business comes from word-of-mouth. We rarely ever do advertising or marketing, nor do we have salespeople. Instead, people share what they like about us, how we are transparent, and how we helped their businesses. Oftentimes, people contact us because they have either read some of my articles or saw other influential people engaging with me via social media. What makes it easy for our clients to share is that they see our enthusiasm for what we do. People aren't going to share your brand if you do not show enthusiasm for your products or services. In essence, people get excited about your brand if you are excited about your brand. At its core, brand building comes down to two key factors, enthusiasm and likability.

Unlike the fast-talking, late-night TV salespeople of years ago, who could sell anything they were handed, today, if you do not show genuine enthusiasm and passion, and truly believe that what you are selling is the best product or best service available, nobody else will either. You can't just think it's okay, you can't think it's just better than others. You need to believe that what you have to offer is the next sliced bread!

Steve Jobs once said of Apple's core values, "We believe people with passion can change the world for the better . . . and that those people who are crazy enough to think they can change the world are the ones who actually do."

Along with that innate confidence in your product or service comes the likability factor. Whether they realize it or not, people talk about and promote brands that they like every day. Whether it's Heineken or Budweiser, Ford cars or Chevy trucks, people talk about, recommend, share, or suggest a brand because they like the company, what they stand for, how they treat their customers, and the products and service they offer. If people don't like you, trust you as a brand, or cannot connect with you, they won't be spreading the word about your brand.

Brand Building: Getting Started

Before you can build a brand today, particularly in social media, you need to understand that you are not there to sell or promote. The people you are reaching out to are not just people with money or those you want to sucker into buying your products or using your services. They are people whom you want to identify with your brand and like what you do and what you stand for. So if you've been indoctrinated to simply sell, sell, sell anything to anyone at any cost, you need to change your mind-set before trying to build a brand via social media.

At the core of brand building is having an understanding of who you are. This will be your identity in the world. If done correctly, your identity will positively influence people. To figure out who you are, start by asking yourself the following questions:

* *What does your business have to offer?* You may be offering products, services, or even wisdom and knowledge about a particular topic. Your business needs something that people can like, which can be anything from designer apparel to home remodeling tips.

- *What does your brand stand for?* This encompasses your beliefs and your passions other than your products or services. For example, are you passionate about being green? About technology? About supporting a particular cause or charity? About government reform?

- *What makes your products, services, or business as a whole different from your competitors?* What can you offer that sets you apart from everyone else? Perhaps you offer unsurpassed technical support; faster, more reliable service; unique one-of-a kind handcrafted items; or a return policy unmatched in your industry.

- *Why are you doing this?* If every entrepreneur were strictly in business to make money, everyone would look at most lucrative industries and launch a business in those fields. Clearly people are in different industries for different reasons. My passion for computers, technology, the web, and helping people led me to

TELL YOUR STORY

You want to be likeable? Tell people the story behind your business. What triggered your desire to start your company? What happened along the way and how did your business grow? You can share your passion and excitement for your brand in your story. Try not to just launch into a story. You tell the story in your communications or by having people click on a link to the About Us page on your website, or ask about other people's or companies' stories. It's all about tactically sharing. People are more likely to follow you if they know who you are and how you got where you are today.

Note: If you're trying to share with someone or with an organization, don't link to a home page where you are selling stuff. It's perceived as trying to trick people into a sales pitch. It doesn't work. If you have a good story to tell, link them directly to your About Us page or your profile on Facebook, LinkedIn, or elsewhere.

launch Fuel Online. Florists had a dream of working with flowers, dance studios are run by people who love dance, actors have a passion for performing, retailers believe their products are the best, and financial advisors love the world of investments. Think about the big picture and why you are passionate about your business and what mark you can leave by doing what you do.

These are all-important questions to answer when you try to brand yourself and your business, especially online and in social media where everything is completely transparent, or should be.

Personal vs. Corporate Brand

Before you can launch your brand, or take your current brand onto social media, you need to determine which direction you are taking, a personal or corporate image. In some cases you will have both. I made the decision not to be a logo and instead decided to be Scott Levy, the guy behind the company. I believe that if you have the opportunity to build a personal brand, you should do it. A lot of businesses fail for reasons beyond their control; people sell or move on to new projects or companies. If you have a personal brand, your followers will be with you, eager to see what you do next. Your personal brand follows you to your next endeavor

This isn't to say a personal brand is for everyone. Many large, established companies do very well without their founder having a strong personal brand. Selling products to a mass market doesn't require it. You buy many products simply because you like them and what the company is all about without knowing anything about the face behind the business. However, like Ray Kroc, of McDonald's fame, or Lee Iacocca, who launched the Ford Mustang before becoming well-known for turning General Motors around, major corporate leaders often have their own personal brand.

For authors, speakers, celebrities, and service professionals who run their own practices, a personal brand is essential. You are the brand and people want to engage with you. Those people who own several businesses also benefit from having a personal brand. Jay-Z is an example of someone who owns a number of businesses, but is better known and has a larger following than the individual businesses he owns. Martha Stewart is the perfect example of a personal brand that outshines her enterprises. And while the Dallas Mavericks of the NBA have a strong fan base, more people know team owner Mark Cuban than are fans of the ball club.

Among the benefits of having a personal brand is that you can more easily connect with people who will relate to you as an individual. They can empathize with you, agree with you, and gain insight into what makes you tick. People root for individuals that they like and admire. As a result, you can gain fans more easily as an individual simply by being transparent and putting yourself out there. You can then use your fan base to support all of your endeavors, which may mean your next book, a new clothing line, or any other enterprise you may start up.

On the other side of the coin, you also fall under a lot of scrutiny when you have a personal brand. People watch your every move very closely, which means your privacy may take a hit. In addition, if you screw up, you are on your own, naked before your fans, having to answer tough questions and bail yourself out. Tiger Woods had no one to help him when his brand took a huge hit after his extramarital affairs began to surface. It is easier to screw up a personal brand than a corporate one, and harder to make amends.

Corporate brands have an identity as a company, which usually takes some of the pressure and responsibility off of any one individual. One goal is obviously to build brand awareness of products and/or services. The other objective, which is so important in social media, is that the corporate brand make a commitment to stand for something. In this regard, corporate brands may have greater resources to make good on such promises. They can sponsor events and activities with a large employee base more easily than personal brands, unless the latter are celebrities.

Corporate brands also are less likely to fall under the microscope and can rebound more easily from negative publicity because the relationship is less personal. While this may not be the case after a major

---

TIPS AND RULES FOR HAVING A PERSONAL AND A BUSINESS BRAND

◆ Be sure that you have a reason for and strategy behind using both.

◆ Be sure to have unique content and thoughts to share on each.

◆ If one brand is already established—either your personal or corporate brand—don't try to establish the other at the exact same time

◆ Let the business be business and your personal brand be personal

◆ Never post personal brand content on the business brand

---

oil spill, companies are more easily forgiven after they make blunders, as illustrated earlier in Chapter 2 when we discussed transparency and the Jet Blue saga. While someone may no longer be a fan of Tiger Woods, they are still likely to buy a product that he formerly endorsed because they still support the product maker's corporate brand, the products it makes, and what the company and its brand stand for.

Having both a personal and corporate brand can be the best of both worlds. This allows you to let people know who is behind the company while also building product awareness. But be careful not to dilute your message, visibility, and brand-building efforts. You certainly can mention cool new products or services, changes you've made in the company, new investments or projects, etc. But it's a balancing act. You can play the brands off each other once in a blue moon for sure, but don't overdo it. You are you, and your persona and personal brand are just that: yours. Your company has its own branding, persona, and methods.

Brand Consistency

Not unlike being transparent, consistency is extremely important when it comes to your brand, personal or corporate. You want to appear to be the same brand with the same ideals on every single platform on which you decide to invest your time. The last thing you want to do is appear

---

ASK THEM TO SHARE YOUR CONTENT

Don't ask people to "like" or share your brand. You want them to do that genuinely.

Instead, ask people to share your content, which in turn generates more quality visibility for your brand. Quality content, such as photos, and news items or information about you or your business gives them something interesting to talk about. Once they share this, they are more likely to "like" the source of the content—which is your brand. People are 10 times more likely to share content when asked to do so. Tip: Keep in mind people are much more likely to share content with their friends or fan base if they think it will help or inspire them, or establish themselves as one of the first to break news or share something truly amazing.

---

to be a fun, exciting, edgy brand with a killer story that is constantly engaging with people on Twitter while having a very stuffy Facebook page where you do not engage with anybody.

The message, the images, the logo, the persona, and everything that supports your brand need to be consistent across all platforms. This doesn't mean you need to use the exact same images on each platform or make the same exact statements. It does, however, mean that the message, the mission, and the voice has to be the same, because people may follow you on multiple, if not all, platforms that you are on. For this reason, I advise people to limit the number of platforms they are on because it's very hard to be good and that consistent on all of them. Unless you have a team working to build and maintain your brand identity, which can be costly, it is time consuming to maintain your brand consistency and engage with your followers on more than a few platforms.

Customer Service and Caring About People

Above and beyond anything else I discuss in this book I want you to emphasize the importance of providing amazing customer service. That is the most significant "take away" you can get. If you adhere to the age-old adage, "The customer is always right" (even when you know they're wrong), you can build one hell of a successful brand, especially on social media. Huge brands have been built overnight because of incredible customer service.

Zappos, the online shoe seller, offers an amazing example of how great customer service can lead to tremendous results. Selling just shoes, something you could buy anywhere and everywhere, Zappos broke the mold. Founded in 1999, under the name Shoesite.com, the Henderson, Nevada, company became Zappos a year later and topped the $1 billion valuation in less than ten years.

Zappos executives recognized that the number-one stumbling block to buying shoes online was the possibility that the shoes would need to be returned and that would cost customers money. With that in mind, Zappos built its brand around extraordinary customer service, offering customers a 365-day, no-cost return policy. It also offered free shipping.

In addition, employees are trained to go the extra mile to help customers on an "unscripted" help line. Zappos employees are taught to do whatever they can to ensure a satisfied customer. It is reported that one customer service professional actually spent eight hours on the phone helping a customer! Reports of Zappos' amazing customer service spread like wildfire across social media, and word-of-mouth became the number-one manner of marketing for the shoe company, which grew by leaps and bounds.

In 2009, Zappos, which now boasts more than 50,000 varieties of shoes, plus handbags and other products, was purchased by Amazon for a deal worth somewhere around $1.2 billion. But the deal was predicated on Zappos' ability to maintain its customer service policies, which it has done. It even has boot camp training courses that teach customer service techniques. If ever there was a company that knew the core value of customer service, Zappos is that company. Its slogan is "Powered by Service," and Zappos' top execs have been quoted as saying, "Everything that we do is focused with our customer in mind. In fact, our call center has an entire team, called quality assurance, which focuses on making sure our customers' experience is the best it can possibly be."

What you can learn from the Zappos story is that if you want to build one hell of a brand, it should feature amazing customer service. Even though you know customers can be annoying, misuse products, or abuse the return policy, you need to instill in your corporate culture that it is important for everyone to take good care of each and every customer. This way they will become a fan of your business and help spread the word via social media. While you may have more returns and may even have to spend a little more money to hire and train employees on how to provide excellent customer service at all times, that investment will pay off one hundredfold when people are talking about how much they love your brand.

At the root of customer service is caring about people. It may sound simple, but it is such an important part of successfully building a brand. Social media has given customers a voice like they have never had before. The nameless, faceless company that didn't really care what the consumer thought of it can't avoid social media visibility today. A customer or potential customer could have 3 or 300,000 followers or know someone who has a massive following. Just as rave reviews about a company can travel quickly across social media, so can stories of rude service or a company being unresponsive to their customers.

Therefore, it is your job on social media to care about people and make them your friends and your fans. You want them to love your brand, share your passion for your company, and spread their enthusiasm across their social media channels. That's how brand champions are created and how you can enjoy an incredible amount of free marketing.

One of my favorite social media success stories is one that belongs to my friend, author, consultant, and entrepreneur Peter Shankman (@PeterShankman on Twitter). Peter was at an airport getting ready to board a plane. Peter, a huge fan of Morton's Steakhouses, was craving some steak and jokingly tweeted about it (see Figure 3–1, page 49).

He really and truly was joking. He boarded the plane, shut off his phone, and 2.5 hours later landed at Newark International Airport. He looked for his driver, saw his name, and waved to him. As Peter greeted the driver, he in turn was greeted by a guy in a tux carrying a Morton's bag. As per Peter's account:

Hey @Mortons - can you meet me at newark airport with a porterhouse when I land in two hours? K, thanks. :)

Figure 3–1 *Peter unwittingly sets up a customer service branding opportunity for Morton's.*

Alex, from Morton's Hackensack, walks up to me, introduces himself, and hands me a bag. He proceeds to tell me that he'd heard I was hungry, and inside is a 24 oz. Porterhouse steak, an order of colossal shrimp, a side of potatoes, one of Morton's famous round things of bread, two napkins, and silverware.

He hands me the bag.

I Was Floored.

So Peter proceeds to tweet out this (see Figure 3–2).

Twitter and social platforms went crazy for the story. Peter was interviewed and told this story numerous times, on major news and

Oh. My. God. I don't believe it. @mortons showed up at EWR WITH A PORTERHOUSE! lockerz.com/s/130578715 # OMFG!

Figure 3–2 *Peter Shankman's now-famous customer service tweet.*

TV networks and at speaking engagements. He also wrote a blog post on Shankman.com: "The Greatest Customer Service Story Ever Told, Starring Morton's Steakhouse," which accrued 251 comments and more than 16,000 shares. Morton's probably received more than $5 million worth of free PR from it.

The moral of the story is that going above and beyond sometimes can give you a hundredfold ROI. Don't expect it to, but if it does, it could make for the greatest customer service story ever told.

But while the Peter Shankman story resulted in a huge positive buzz for Mortons, another eatery found out what it was like to invoke the wrath of social media mavens. In early 2012, an Applebee's restaurant in St. Louis fired an employee for posting a photo of a customer's receipt on the social media site Reddit. The customer, a local pastor, had crossed out the 18 percent service charge added to checks for parties of eight or more and wrote, *"I give God 10% why do you get 18."*

The server's firing soon set off a firestorm on Twitter and Facebook, where thousands of users let Applebee's know that they would boycott the restaurant unless the woman was re-hired. To make matters worse, Applebee's tried to defend its policy of protecting customers' privacy, which posters noted came less than two weeks after the restaurant posted a picture of a note from a guest that clearly revealed the guest's name.

Within hours of the server's initial post on Reddit, there were roughly 17,000 comments on Applebee's original Facebook status noting it had taken "disciplinary action with the team member for violating their guest's right to privacy." Then, to add more fuel to the fire, someone on behalf of Applebee's started deleting some postings while engaging in arguments with other posters, which spilled over onto Twitter. In time, the clamor calmed down, but Applebee's learned the hard way not to provoke the social media faithful.

Branding Via Your Corporate Culture

Another reason for Zappos' unparalleled success is its corporate culture, which includes providing employees with free lunches, free health care, and an atmosphere that encourages the 1,500+ staffers to take down-time to "goof off" outside of the office during their workday. This creates an enthusiasm among employees unmatched by most companies.

Morale-boosting is nothing new in the business world, but today, enthusiasm in the workplace translates to social media posts by employees and customers. It shows in the way people talk and text about your business. If, for example, you are in a restaurant and the server is in a bad mood and not treating you well, you may not only complain to the manager, or not return to the eatery, but you can also talk about it in conversations with your followers or post an online restaurant review. In many instances news of bad service or poor-quality products travels more quickly than positive reviews. Of course, if the server was particularly enthusiastic, friendly, and told you about the specials and some of the best choices on the menu, you might have had a different experience and that can translate to sharing it with your friends and followers. This is true all throughout the business world. Enthusiasm, passion, and love for your brand by managers, salespeople, technical help, or any kind of service providers is contagious. When people are enthusiastic about what they do and they believe in the products they make and/or sell, doesn't it make a believer out of you? Don't you want to tell other people? Therefore, it is important to care about the people with whom you work and develop a positive corporate culture that shows up in your brand.

Your corporate culture should also illustrate your view of the world around you. This is where green companies can make a strong impact, along with companies that provide their employees with a caring environment. Good employee health policies; medical screenings; maternity, paternity, and adoption leave; as well as child care, education tuition, and so much more can be part of a caring corporate culture. This results in a win-win situation. First you have happy and enthusiastic employees who love their jobs, and they in turn treat your customers like gold . . . as they should. Your customers are happy to do business with such enthusiastic employees and share your brand.

Identification with customers can also create a strong connection between corporate culture and brand awareness. For example, *Business*

Week wrote a feature article in February 2010 that explained how insurance and financial giant USAA, based in San Antonio, Texas, became so successful at customer relations with their extensive client base of active and retired members of the military and their families. The article talked about how the 13,000 customer reps who communicate by phone or the internet with their clients are empathetic and in touch with the needs of military personnel and their families. During their training, USAA service reps read letters of deployment, eat MRE's ("meals ready to eat," for soldiers), read letters from soldiers in the field to their families back home, and even walk around wearing 65-pound backpacks to get a feel for the soldier's experiences. As a result, service reps care that much more deeply about their clients, and those clients share that caring with other military families.

In the end, it becomes so much easier to create a strong corporate culture when it is based on the simple principle of really caring for people. Whether you are on Facebook, Twitter, LinkedIn, or the next great platform, you need to care about people and treat them as if they will be your next business partner, boyfriend, girlfriend, or best friend.

Brand Visibility: Techniques and Tactics

Your brand becomes visible by being shared, read, and seen on social media, as well as on traditional media. From logos to slogans to photos to tweets, posts, and advertising, your message must be consistent.

In an effort to create consistency, you will want to write down your brand objectives and consider your reasons behind building a brand. You will review the benefits and highlights of the products and/or service you offer, review what makes your business unique (which may tie into your corporate culture), and think about your motives for being in business. You will then add to your answers the final ingredient: Who are your target customers and what do they want? This question can be answered largely by engaging with like-minded individuals on social media. For example, if you are planning to open a new brewery, you'll want to find out not only whether people want lighter beers, but also healthier ingredients? Better packaging? Greener packaging? Locally brewed beers? Darker beers?

The more you learn, the easier it will be to create a brand that generates a following.

Your Toolbox

To build a consistent brand, you'll want to have:

- A slogan and/or tagline that is easy to remember and conveys your brand and/or your strength (what makes you different) in a single line.
- A logo that is easy to identify and visually depicts what your brand is all about.
- Images and/or videos that highlight your company culture, your products or services, as well as the people (or person) behind the logo. The images should be consistent, for example, a brand selling retro clothing might want to have a retro look in all of their photos, perhaps in black and white.
- A list of attributes so that whoever is promoting your brand for your business will feature the same characteristics in outgoing messages.
- A consistent voice and tone so that your brand is conveyed in the same manner: upbeat, heartfelt, homespun, sexy, or even comical, depending on what you are trying to convey. Clearly Louie Anderson and Kendra Wilkerson are conveying different messages in their personal brands, and the voice of their postings or tweets will differ, as would those for Chuck E. Cheese and Oracle.

Color choices can also create very different images. The colors for a fast food place that caters to children will differ from that of a law firm that specializes in wills and estates. Look closely at choices of colors to determine what you believe they convey.

Brand integration means that all of the above need to be in sync. A funny, cheerful, kid-friendly logo with dreary colors and a very serious heartfelt message could be very confusing. Keep everything coordinated for brand consistency.

Before building a brand, you need to think about it carefully. You want to make sure you are going to present a clear, concise, and consistent message. It's very difficult to switch gears midway through. People want to know what your brand is all about and who you are. If you confuse them with inconsistent or mixed messages, you will lose them as followers, fans, and ultimately, as customers.

Chapter 4

Convergence Strategies and Your Social Media Team

Convergence describes how numerous forms of media are becoming integrated. It's about smartphones, apps, and various mobile devices that have made it possible to watch TV shows on computers and movies on your iPhone and have your Facebook friends also find you on Pinterest or LinkedIn, and vice versa. Links between websites and social media platforms are abundant, and people now are utilizing all sorts of tools and platforms at the same time. As a result, companies are now branding and marketing in ways that best integrate the power and potential of the different forms of media. TV programs like ABC's hit series *Dancing With the Stars* are asking people to tweet their votes, hosting blogs about the dancers, having discussions on their Facebook page, and showing snippets of dances on YouTube.

The idea of convergence is to have people see your brand wherever they are. On social media, it's about engaging with the user and providing them with something of value. Convergence is the end result of a social media strategy encompassing several platforms. Your current and future customers may be using one or several of these platforms, and you want them to see your brand appearing on several platforms with links connecting your Twitter account to your Facebook page, your Facebook page to your videos on YouTube, and so on. Of course, this doesn't just happen by posting a few links. There is a method behind the madness, and that takes careful planning.

The Road to Convergence

To build, or maintain, brand awareness on social media, it's critical that you develop a complete and in-depth strategy in advance based on your goals—whether it's to sell or introduce products and services, provide customer service, or build your brand. Your goals will guide your decision on which platforms to use and for what purposes. For example, if you are an outdoor gear manufacturer looking to introduce a new style of back-pack, you might want to use Twitter or Facebook for crowdsourcing to get your followers' ideas on what colors you should offer or what's most important to them in terms of design and features. You could also pin on Pinterest some outstanding photos of the product in amazing outdoor locations, using the colors selected by your fans and followers.

If you own a retail cutlery business, you could demonstrate your latest knives in YouTube videos showing them slicing through rope, coins, a book, a block of wood, etc. You could then use Twitter to crowdsource ideas for what people want to see next, or to spread the word: "Check out the cutting power of our amazing knives on our YouTube channel," and use your business's Facebook page to start a conversation about experiences with "knives that just didn't cut it." All these platforms would link to one another and to your website, where you would offer incredible customer service policies, and perhaps a blog. You could share comments from customers and from viewers of your videos via Facebook and Twitter. This way, you utilize each platform to serve a different purpose, from visual demonstrations to comments on great customer service. This is an integrated social media strategy.

Keep in mind that most businesses can't be good on every platform, so pick the platforms that best meet your needs. Then consider your bandwidth, manpower, and budget to decide how many of those platforms you can develop and maintain at a high level. It's really not that complex from a technical standpoint to execute such a strategy. The links are simple to put in place. What is much more important is to make the most of each platform you use and to have a plan to cross-promote and utilize them. Ask yourself: Why am I using each platform and how can I benefit from what this platform offers? Can I provide something of value in 140 characters on Twitter, or am I better served by posting photos on Pinterest? Can I do both? If you are on a platform just for the sake of having a presence there, don't bother; you'll be wasting your time and money. The last thing you want to do is have a social account representing your brand and for it to suck! Only do it if you're going to do it right, and it makes sense.

Integration Is a Beautiful Thing for Sephora

Since its birth in France in 1970 to 1,300 stores in 27 countries today, Sephora has become a world leader in the beauty, fragrance, skin-care, and hair-care industries.

To continue building brand awareness, Sephora's social media and business goals include gaining a larger fan base and customer base as well as positioning itself as the leader and expert in beauty. With their demographic research showing a large customer base of women ages 20 to 35, the company decided to feature its products in beautiful photos on both Pinterest and Facebook. It also uses Twitter to spread the word about products, news, and expertise in personal beauty.

The company's social media activities include engaging a community of 5 million Facebook fans and 900,000 Twitter followers, as well as a strong presence on Pinterest. It keeps customers apprised of new products and promotions such as "Fan Friday," which it considers a "customer-listening channel."

Pinterest has become a significant source of sales, with its users spending 15 percent more than Sephora's Facebook fans, Sephora's chief of digital (CDO) Julie Bornstein noted. She says that while Pinterest users are generally more interested in purchasing products, Facebook serves as an important customer engagement tool, providing Sephora with a barometer of customer likes and dislikes.

WHY SEPHORA CHOSE ITS PLATFORMS

- Fans connect with each other about Sephora
- It gets real-time, raw reactions from customers
- On Facebook, Sephora can target women demographically for upcoming events

A "15 Days of Beauty Thrills" giveaway in 2012 through Facebook, Twitter, and Pinterest drew a significant response. Sephora then incentivized people to "Like" its Facebook page by offering to give them earlier access to the next day's "thrill." As a result, Sephora's fan base grew six times the normal rate, and more sales were linked to Facebook than ever before. Sephora also integrates various sites including Tumblr and YouTube into its mobile apps and includes "Pin It" buttons on every Pinterest product page,

Figure 4–1 *Sephora's Facebook page.*

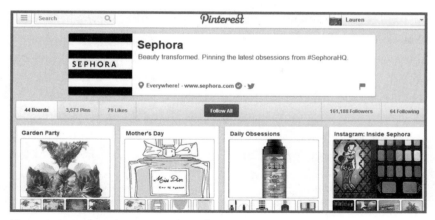

Figure 4–2 *Sephora's Pinterest board.*

Another way Sephora increases sales and brand awareness is to focus on Apple Passbook users, who are some of Sephora's best customers: Users are notified when they are near a store and can purchase products using gift cards and loyalty cards. More than 600,000 have registered Sephora's Beauty Insider loyalty cards in their iPhone mobile wallets. Sephora also developed Sephora To Go, a mobile checkout app, which delivers product reviews, as well as new products and personalized information about previous interactions. Sephora was ranked number one in "Mobile IQ" by the L2 analyst group (http://www.forbes.com/sites/lydiadishman/2012/04/09/sephoras-smart-social-and-digital-makeover/).

Lowe's Builds Something Better with Pinterest and Facebook

When Lowe's started in 1946 as a single hardware store, the original founders never could have imagined that they would one day have more than 1,750 retail locations and be engaging in something called "social media" with customers worldwide.

Today, while serving more than 15 million customers each week, Lowe's social media goal has become to engage and attract more women customers, because women are the household decision-makers. With that as a primary target market for social media engagement, Lowe's chose to utilize Pinterest to home in on the platform's predominantly 25- to 35-year-old female demographic. It also wanted to utilize the massive female market on Facebook to build greater brand awareness. By integrating Facebook (see Figure 4–3) and Pinterest (see Figure 4–4)—it used similar designs and color palette to maintain brand consistency across the platforms—Lowe's was able to reach this target audience. Some of the results:

- More than 1.1 million likes on Facebook, twice that of rival Home Depot
- A 32-percent increase in followers, thanks to a Pinterest tab on Facebook (Facebook tabs have since been eliminated, replaced essentially with apps)
- 3.6 million followers on Pinterest, up from just 7,000 exactly one year ago

How Lowe's Increased Sales and Brand Awareness

- Lowe's social media team answers customer questions on Facebook and Twitter within minutes.

Figure 4–3 *Lowe's Facebook page.*

Figure 4–4 *Lowe's Pinterest board.*

- The team takes negative questions and comments offline by asking users to send an email.
- Lowe's launched a Vine mobile app and a Facebook app to show "Fix in Six" videos of quick project tips for consumers.

24/7 . . . or Not

Social media platforms are 24/7 and global—so it's the middle of the business day somewhere. That means you've got the opportunity to win new fans or brand champions and drive traffic and sales to your website anytime, day or night. Of course, maintaining your presence on social media 24/7 is not easy. One of my biggest pet peeves is the idea of being automated to stay active at all times. Having a piece of software automatically tweeting out messages or posting Facebook status updates when there's no one manning your social media platforms doesn't allow for the interaction that makes these social platforms. If someone asks a question, starts a conversation, or needs customer service, you have nobody there to provide a prompt response, which defeats the purpose of social media. It's kind of like when someone sends you a text message, and you reply right away; you know they are there because they just sent you that text seconds ago and probably have their phone in their hand. So when it takes them three hours to reply to your text, it probably ticks you off.

If you want to have a 24/7 presence on social media, you need to have people on your social media team working in shifts. Some Fortune 500 companies have round-the-clock social media teams. They understand the value of customer service, likely have a global presence, and know that being a likeable, human company is everything. You achieve that likability by having quick answers and by helping people who are upset or distraught or can't figure something out. You become their hero by having someone there to help them at 2 A.M.

Of course, many businesses cannot afford 24/7 staffing. So simply make clear on your website and social media platforms the hours during which you'll handle and respond to customer service inquiries and other postings.

Your Target Market: Demographics

Knowing and understanding your target customers is essential in all forms of marketing, and factors into how you represent yourself in the media. Today, numerous research tools allow you to zero in on your audience. It's critical that you know there's an audience for what you are selling and have insights as to who makes up this audience, especially if you are entering a crowded market.

One of the most basic methods is to use Twitter's search function, which will return people using that term in their tweets. If you use just the word, then you'll get both the word and people using it as a hashtag. However, if you search a hashtag, then you will get results for just the hashtag. The next step up would be using something like Google Alerts, where you can set up custom alerts for any specific mentions of your brand or niche you're trying to monitor. If you want to monitor conversation in real time, add a column to TweetDeck, Hootsuite, or whatever social media management system you're using for those keywords. There are also more complex, detailed platforms that usually charge a fee such as Sprout Social, Topsy, Trackur, and radian6. Those are all pretty solid, advanced tools. Companies investing millions into their social budgets that want to take it to the next level can even have tools custom built. We use a combination of all these, plus our own proprietary, custom tools.

Having demographic information on your current customers and an idea of your most likely potential customers will factor into your decision on which social media sites to use and how to engage. For example, if you know what keywords interest your target audience, you can monitor Twitter conversations that use those keywords or hashtags. On most platforms you can also look for discussions or groups in which you are likely to find your demographic market. You want to research which platforms are most effective in reaching your audience. This way you can minimize your costs while improving your conversion rates and hopefully generate more leads and sales.

For example, if you're a vacation destination for weddings and your research shows that keywords and phrases such as "wedding locations" and "wedding planning" show up more frequently on Pinterest than on other platforms, you might be inclined to consider that platform. Things and places with beautiful, powerful imagery do very well on Pinterest. If the demographics also show a significant number of women age 20 to 35 using Pinterest, and that's your demographic, then you will certainly want to use powerful visuals on Pinterest as one of your primary social media platforms and post powerful visuals. You would start by allocating a portion of your budget and manpower to preparing the graphics you'll need to make a splash on Pinterest. You'll also allocate funding to have a team ready to respond to and engage with your Pinterest followers. You may then determine that the second biggest audience for your business is on Facebook, so you will utilize your Facebook page to engage customers, ask questions about wedding plans, and perhaps even run a contest.

If you have been marketing to your target audience for years, you will have a better idea of who you are going after. It is then a matter of figuring out where your customers spend their time on social media. Don't make assumptions. Look at the statistics available from each

WHEN TO HIRE AN OUTSIDE SOCIAL MEDIA TEAM

The decision to hire an outside firm to manage your company's social media is a crucial one, and there are pluses and minuses. But before you go there, ask yourself: Do I know enough and have the time to hire and manage a social media manager? You need to know what to expect of a manager, if the applicant is telling the truth, and if you're getting what you could and should be getting out of social media. If you don't, then it's best to hire an outside firm. Chances are that you don't have the time, understanding, or the right people to manage and execute your social media strategy in house. You also may not have the passion for it.

For example, even though you may have people in-house who can design or hire high-level designers for your website, if yours is not a web design firm, it's unlikely you could do a better job than a dedicated, passionate web design firm that eats and breathes design. Plus, a company with multiple clients has seen more, done more brainstorming, more research and analysis, and learned from more mistakes than you'll ever know. A dedicated social media company gives you access to many more minds and a lot more experience. You may have access to a team of five to ten people for the price of one or two staffers.

The downside to hiring an outside firm is picking the wrong one. You need to know enough to ask the right questions to vet the many self-proclaimed media gurus and experts out there. Hiring the wrong firm or person can potentially do more damage than good, while also draining your budget. Find out exactly what they are doing for your company and how often they work on your stuff. Seek out a high-quality reputable firm that is honest with you; beware of companies that are primarily marketing and sales machines that outsource your work to other companies or that only have sales people trying to close a deal. If it smells like snake oil, it probably is.

Therefore, before hiring an outside social media company, ask for references. Just as word-of-mouth marketing is an asset to sales, it is also important for you to learn about social media companies. Ask around and get some recommendations from business owners who have worked with these companies. Find out the costs and the results.

social media platform as well as from any of the many companies that collect web data such as Alexa, which ranks 30 million websites worldwide and provides demographic information.

By reviewing any of the wealth of available demographics, you will not only find numbers of followers but also age, income levels, interests, and so much more. You will also see the trends that social media platforms have taken in recent years. For example, Facebook was once primarily used by college students and a "younger" audience. Not anymore. Today, many kids are creating new excuses *not* to friend their parents and even grandparents, who have all taken to using Facebook, making it one of the two most used websites in the world, along with Google.

Of course, part of your research is to zero in on influencers in your field, who can help you build an enormous following and serve as your brand champions. Search for the leading bloggers or influencers in your field and use tools like Kred, Klout, PeerIndex, and WeFollow to find social media influencers.

Preparation and Policies

Before you launch your social media campaigns, you must have policies in place and your team must be aware of them and, more importantly, abide by them. For example, how are you going to handle rude comments, negativity, or trolls? What will you do in case of a crisis? If you are on the verge of a PR nightmare, you need to have people ready and able to make decisions, sometimes very quickly. This might mean issuing a well-timed apology or publicly illustrating how you solved a major problem or put out a fire. You need a damage-control plan, or as I call it, a "break glass in case of emergency" plan.

Some companies have several people review social media communications before they go out to minimize any social media disasters. Too many companies have learned the importance of a system of checks and balances the hard way, such as when Chrysler hired an outside agency to handle its social media and someone tweeted on the @ChryslerAutos account, "I find it ironic that Detroit is known

RULES AND GUIDELINES TO CONSIDER

Some rules you might want to include in your social media policy:

◆ You must be at least 18 years of age to post on any of the company's social media sites.

◆ You are prohibited from posting personal information about any client or customer of the company or its affiliates.

◆ You will not post material that infringes on copyright, trademark, or patents owned by a third party.

◆ You will not post material considered sensitive or proprietary to the company or its affiliates.

◆ You will not post material that is considered slanderous, libelous, or hurtful to another person or business.

◆ You will not post any material that could be considered profanity or discriminatory.

◆ You will never use inappropriate language, harass, or threaten anyone.

◆ You will not engage in personal business or discuss personal issues of any kind.

◆ You will not post, tweet, or send out knowingly false statements or provide inaccurate information on any social media platforms.

◆ Policies may be updated by the company or social media manager at any time. New policies will be distributed to all team members.

◆ Failure to adhere to all policies may result in termination.

Along with strict policies, guidelines might include:

◆ Always try to be authentic and transparent on behalf of the brand in anything you send out.

◆ Support claims with appropriate links to information if possible.

RULES AND GUIDELINES TO CONSIDER, CONTINUED

◆ Always show customers that you care about them and are willing to go the extra mile for them.

◆ Be polite and do not engage in arguments with customers even if provoked. If you disagree with the opinions of others, do so respectfully.

◆ If you are not a customer service representative, make sure to promptly forward all customer service questions, complaints, and issues to someone who is.

◆ Speak in a polite, courteous manner, and avoid "corporate speak" or "technical jargon."

◆ Try to add value. Provide worthwhile information and perspective.

◆ Always be honest and use your best judgment in all situations.

◆ Avoid plagiarism at all costs. Document all sources and give credit where credit is due.

◆ Participate, don't promote.

◆ When in doubt, ask for help/clarification.

Take your time and make a concerted effort to consider all possible scenarios and create policies and/or guidelines that can help you avoid, or at least minimize, as many potential problems as possible. While you'd like to say "use common sense" in hopes of covering many of these areas, it is to your benefit to have everything spelled out, especially if someone does break the rules and you need to take some sort of action, which could range from moving them off a certain platform to termination.

---

as the #motorcity and yet no one here knows how to f@#$ing drive." Apparently the agency representative thought he was being clever on his own Twitter account, but sent it accidentally on the company's account instead. Angry Detroit motorists responded, causing Chrysler plenty of PR headaches and putting the social media agency representative out of a job. A policy clearly barring employees from using their own Twitter account while at work—which was what the employee thought he was doing—or that each post must be reviewed by another team member prior to sending could have prevented this PR disaster.

If you hire an outside firm to handle your social media, you still need to have very carefully worded policies in place covering anyone working on your account, and holding them responsible if they don't adhere to such policies.

Many companies have posted social media policies online, so rather than reinvent the wheel, review them for an idea of rules that you may want to include in your own policy. There are generic rules that simply make good sense and others that will fit your company more closely. Put them in writing and make them available to everyone on your social media team. It can save you headaches in the long run.

Your Social Media Team

Convergence and strategies will never take shape if you don't have a team to implement them. Social media "teams" range from one person in a small company to hundreds of employees in a major corporation. They can be part of the marketing division, public relations department, or a specific team hired solely to handle social media. Today, the marketing efforts of some companies are nothing but social media.

Every company structures its social media team differently. Most companies wind up with social media managers; in bigger corporations, these managers may report to the directors of advertising or marketing. Regardless of structure, someone needs to lead the way and take charge of social media output

Your social media manager's level of responsibility will depend on how experienced they are with social media, the size of your team, and the size and reach of the company. Obviously the one-person team has to take on the full load, so it may be smart to limit the number of platforms that you can cover well so that your manager can respond to people promptly and post accordingly. If you don't have the budget or manpower to be on several platforms, then stick with the top one or two on your list, the ones that best meet your needs and are used by your target audience.

Hiring the Right Players

You need to select the right people for the right tasks and train them. If your focus is solely on branding, they'll require less training than someone focused on customer service, because branding generally requires less direct interaction with fans and followers and has fewer "urgent" problems to solve. Nonetheless, it's almost impossible not to get into some degree of customer service, because you are still engaging with numerous people.

It's also important to note that many human resources professionals aren't well versed in hiring people to work in social media. It's a new

TEN WAYS TO MOTIVATE AND EMPOWER YOUR TEAM

1. Make sure that they know the product inside and out, and have seen or used it.

2. Make sure they know that all engagement with the public is reviewed.

3. Celebrate team members who go the extra mile for customers.

4. Reward team members who thought outside the box and solved problems.

5. Promote culture, fun, passion, and happiness.

6. Incentivize them by offering prizes and bonuses for outstanding work and meeting objectives.

7. Train your team to turn complaints into customers or fans.

8. Empower them to solve problems and make customers raving fans.

9. Document your team's amazing ideas and successes and share it with them.

10. Let them be human and give them free time. Try using Google's strategy of letting employees devote 20 percent of their time to company-related projects that interest them personally.

field and a different animal than marketing. So you may want to bring in an outside expert to help in the hiring process, at least when choosing your social media manager. I've been called in to help HR people in the hiring of social media teams; not to do their jobs for them, but to lend some expertise in the field.

You'll find that most people who want to work in social media are familiar with Facebook, Twitter, and perhaps LinkedIn, and have been on YouTube. Their home use is fine, but representing a business is another matter entirely. For example, the language they may use with friends, off-color jokes they may send, or their trash talk about a celebrity or a business clearly isn't suitable for your business. They must be ready, willing, and enthusiastic about learning about your business, your products, and your services. They will need to absorb a lot of information about the company and be very good listeners. It's like hiring a salesperson who has to know all about the lawnmower or SUV before he can sell it or market it. While they're on your platforms, each team member's social media identity must be that of your business and brand. They need to make sure that your followers, fans, and customers are happy, and you need to motivate and empower them to make people happy.

Your Dream Team

- *People who are social media savvy*. You want people who are comfortable on at least one social media platform, and preferably more. Because everyone claims to be an "expert" because they spend time on Facebook, ask tough how-to questions, as well as what they might do in a certain scenario. You can tell in 30 seconds if someone knows about social media or is making it up as they go. If you ask the candidate what they thought of the new (and fictitious) social network "Fourblog," and they punt with something like, "I can't believe how fast it's growing!" you know they're not being honest. An honest person will admit to knowing about only one platform, for example, yet may be terrific on that platform and valuable to the company.

- *Knowledgeable team members.* Make sure everyone is very well versed in what your business does, its products or services, and the brand you are trying to convey. If they don't know an answer to a customer or follower's query, make sure they know where to find it quickly. Nothing is worse than giving people wrong answers or no answers. Knowledgeable customer service is vital because it represents the business and helps build trust. It also leaves a lasting impression.

- *The right people in the right positions.* Patience and the ability to remain calm even in situations where people are nasty, obnoxious, or just plain rude are important attributes if you are going to handle customer service. People who aren't as comfortable engaging on a steady basis but have terrific design or graphic skills may be marvelous designing the look of your pages and choosing the best images. Utilize the various skills people bring to the team accordingly.

- *The right people on the right platforms.* Your Twitter platform will need people ready to think fast and respond quickly, because Twitter is an ongoing conversation. Facebook customer service reps will have a little more time to respond, so you may have people who are better at research and giving more detailed answers handling your Facebook page. If someone is more visually oriented and excels in video production, put them on your YouTube platform.

- *Interaction and consistency.* You have a brand and a social media voice (and tone) to present that brand. Some businesses are more lighthearted, others emphasize their culture and history; some are trendy, and others are more elegant or refined. The brand and the voice need to be in sync and consistent from platform to platform. Therefore, your team members must interact with one another to make sure everyone is on the same page. Meetings to brief everyone on the latest news and activities are also vital so that fans and followers get the same overall message from each platform and in a manner to which they are accustomed, even if the actual words and images differ.

- *Out-of-the-box thinking within the box.* Your style and your message are encompassed in your overall brand. But within that box, you do not want everyone saying and doing the exact same thing, reading from scripts or putting up the same posts like robots. Empower people to be creative, think out of the box, and come up with new and innovative solutions within the brand and company parameters.

- *People who help one another.* Rather than throwing new employees into the fray, have them team up and work with more experienced staffers who can help them decide what to post or how to respond before they do it on their own. Handholding is welcome on a good social media team. The same holds true for the team's technical and design members. Encourage people to learn from one another and ask questions.

- *A team that knows and follows your own best practices.* You may already have well-established working solutions that have served customers well. So make sure your team knows the manner in which things have been done successfully in the past and to use such solutions when necessary, because many problems and customer questions will come up again and again and again.

- *Caring and enthusiasm.* You want a team who genuinely likes what they do and cares about the people with whom they are engaging. The goal of social media is engagement, and you want everyone to have a positive experience when dealing with your business and your brand. Caring and enthusiasm creates a positive experience, especially when someone on your team goes above and beyond for a customer or potential customer.

- *Honesty.* You want your team members to be honest when engaging on social media and not to make up stories or lie when answering a question. You also want team members to be honest with you, or with their social media manager.

Social media can be exhausting, especially for those doing customer service for hours at a time. If someone cannot handle the schedule, they should discuss it with their manager and perhaps work a different shift or fewer hours. If they are not comfortable in the position, they should ask if they can be moved to another job. A good social media team, like any team in business, has to communicate and let the manager know if there are problems or concerns, whether they are personal or with the platforms on which they are working.

Chapter 5

Ways to Engage

Facebook considers being engaged when someone clicks anywhere on your posting, while *Bloomberg BusinessWeek* journalist Bernhard Warner calls engagement "the new currency for social marketing effectiveness." I believe engagement is when you can seduce an action or conversation out of your viewers. However you define it, knowing how to engage successfully on one or several platforms is the key to utilizing social media to reach your business and branding goals.

Engagement comes in a variety of forms, from liking to retweeting to answering questions and solving problems via social media. The ways to engage on each platform are different, but the concept is the same. You want what you have to say to resonate with the recipient so that he or she is prompted to respond in some manner, from joining a conversation to asking a question or answering one. You also want to have something valuable to say, something organic and authentic that represents your brand in a way that interests people. In fact, while it is very important that people like you, even the act of "liking" on Facebook is becoming a bit passé, and those endorsements that LinkedIn keeps asking that you give your connections are becoming a bit forced. You want genuine interest and people who really want to engage. Retweeting or sharing content, for example, is a follower's own choice and has greater significance because they are sending something of value—their personal endorsement and all the demographics that go with it, as well as the possibility of gaining new followers from their list.

Finding Your Audience

Before engaging on any platform, you need to determine who makes up your target audience. The overall marketplace is segmented with numerous niche markets and you need to identify yours. You can dig deeper than ever before when researching demographics today. You can use tools like Google Analytics to see exactly where visitors are coming from and how long they are staying on each page. You can determine what people are liking most on your Facebook page and compile some of your own audience demographics. If you're just starting out, you need to identify prospective clients with whom you will engage.

Platforms such as Facebook offer tools like "Insights" with interest graphs and social graphs that compile the interests of the user and data from his or her friends. So if a 24-year-old male has an interest in soccer and socializes with numerous other soccer enthusiasts, a sporting goods business might target him and his friends. As you seek out data, you can hone it to your region, city, or county. In some instances, you may even find that certain products are well liked in areas far from your location. One clothing retailer in Baltimore sells certain styles, colors, and brands of apparel, thanks to Facebook, to buyers in Europe who happen to like that particular style. Demographics can help you find your target audience, or in some cases discover new customers in other parts of the world.

KLOUT AND KRED SCORES

A person's Kred or Klout score indicates to some degree how influential they are across a variety of social media networks. Klout scores are between 1 and 100; the higher the score, the more influential someone is. Justin Beiber and Barak Obama, for example, have scores in the 90s.

Kred scores measure both influence and outreach, such as community involvement. Outreach on Twitter by retweets, replies, and mentions of others are included; by linking your Facebook account to your Kred profile, you can get outreach points for interactions on your own wall and the walls of other users who have registered their Facebook account with Kred. Kred score interactions include posts, mentions, comments, and likes. Kred influence scores go up to 1,000 points, while outreach scores usually fall between 1 and 10, although this metric apparently has no cap, as scores of 12 have been reported.

Using demographics such as these and those found at numerous other sites can help you zero in on your potential target market. You can also look for influencers on the various sites and check out their Klout or Kred scores to determine if they're influential to the audience with whom you want to engage.

Looking at the Numbers

So how popular is Facebook compared to the other social media platforms? As of December 2012, according to interviews conducted by Pew Research Center's Internet and Life Project, the percentage of internet users on Facebook was more than the next four platforms combined. Facebook's 67 percent topped Twitter at 16 percent, Pinterest at 15 percent, Instagram at 13 percent, and Tumblr at 6 percent, or a combined total of 50 percent between the four next in line behind Facebook. You can see how prevalent Facebook really is in Figure 5–1.

If you're thinking about your demographic audience, then it's important to take a closer look at who uses these popular platforms.

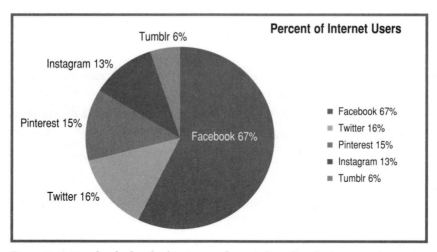

Figure 5–1 *Facebook clearly dominates the social media platforms and is typically ranked second only to Google in the most visited websites worldwide.*

Facebook, for example, is used by 72 percent of women on the internet, while 62 percent of men have Facebook pages. The highest percentage of users fall between ages 18 and 29 at 85 percent, with 30- to 49-year-olds checking in at 73 percent. But for those of you who think Facebook is for the young at heart, consider that 57 percent of internet users between ages 50 and 64 also use Facebook. The age comparison of users between Facebook and Twitter is shown in Figure 5–2.

Twitter, meanwhile, has a slightly higher number of men than women on board with 17 percent of male internet users topping 15 percent of female internet users. There is also an interesting race/ethnic breakdown with black, non-Hispanics checking in at 26 percent, 19 percent for Hispanic users, and white, non-Hispanic users at 14 percent. Here, too, the largest percentage of users are the 18- to 29-year-olds at 27 percent, with a drop-off to 16 percent in the 30- to 49-year-old range.

And if you are visually minded and thinking of utilizing Pinterest to reach your target market, you'd best be thinking about reaching out to the ladies, since 25 percent of women on the internet are on Pinterest compared to only 5 percent of men. See Figure 5–3 for the gender breakdown on Facebook, Twitter, and Pinterest. You'll also find that

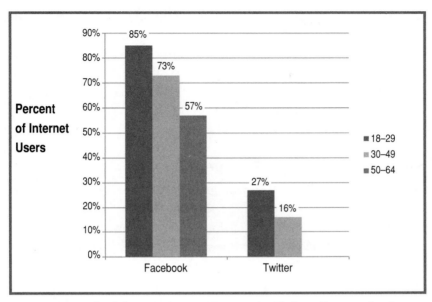

Figure 5–2 *Facebook has an amazing presence with the college market but also with the over-50 market, which is negligible on most other social media platforms.*

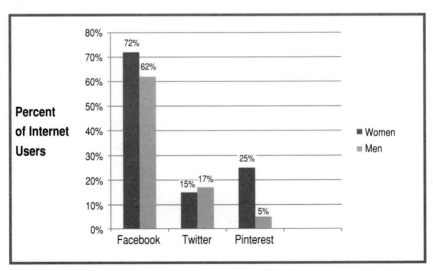

Figure 5–3 *While the percentage of male to female users is close on Facebook and Twitter, there is a major discrepancy on Pinterest.*

there is a peak in the higher income levels for Pinterest, with 23 percent of the audience earning in the $50,000 to $74,999 range per household while the other platforms mentioned are fairly consistent across income lines. Pinterest also has a higher percentage of their users coming from rural communities, while both Facebook and Twitter get more of their audience from the urban areas.

Steps to Encourage Engagement

Once you have established who makes up your target audience, you need to establish your brand identity. Remember, social media allows companies to humanize themselves by how they respond to their audience. Having a brand personality makes it easy for people to relate to your business. Such a personality should remain consistent across all platforms and be distinctive. For example, your brand may be uplifting, fun, and always entertaining to your followers. Perhaps you are the voice of knowledge and reason, respected and typically sharing information that others find fascinating. You may be the high-end trendsetter, always presenting class and elegance. Conversely, you might be the deal maven, always finding a cheaper alternative or way to find a bargain. People get to know and connect with the personality behind the brand, which is why consistency is so important. Of course, whatever you do, you still want to relate to your industry or your field.

Once you've identified your audience and their key channels, you can scan and monitor social media for conversations on specific topics. For example, if you are in the travel industry specializing in extreme sports vacations, you'd type "extreme sports" on the Twitter search bar and find conversations taking place worldwide. This gives you an opportunity to jump into the conversation and engage, not as a salesperson, but as someone with expertise who can help others or provide insights. For example, if people are discussing places for extreme sports activities in Colorado, you can point out a few that perhaps they hadn't thought of, and just like that, you are someone with whom they want to engage. And they may retweet your suggestion to their followers, be it 50 or 5,000. Likewise, search for the hashtag #extremesports on Twitter, and you'll find people who both use the phrase and the hashtag in their tweets so that like-minded users can find them. You can search for groups or pages on Facebook or LinkedIn, or find people talking about the topic you chose on any social media platform and jump into the conversations.

You can also encourage people, via your social media and traditional marketing efforts, to ask questions about your brand or tap into your expertise on a subject. While engaging, you—or whoever is engaging with users on your company's behalf—must always wear your customer service hat and position the company as likeable and helpful. Anyone engaging on your behalf must be well versed in your company and its products and services. If they can't answer a question, they need to know how to find the answer, and fast!

Content Is King

On your own social media pages, there are at least 1,000 ways to get people to engage, such as asking questions, offering daily tips, or posting quotes and fun facts. You should post video and photos: Pictures and videos are shared 40 percent more than text. Contests can be a tremendous way to engage for two reasons: People like the idea of winning something, and if you give away a $100 or $200 prize and 10,000 people have shared or retweeted your post and spread the word about the contest, you win.

You want to put content out there that is useful, helpful, and makes you a resource or reference; you're essentially baiting people to participate. So your content must be clever, creative, entertaining, and, perhaps, a little controversial. You want to achieve that wow factor that comes from people seeing something new and unusual that they then want to share with others.

You need to devise a plan that incorporates all forms of content: conversation, pictures, videos, blogs, and links between your platform and your website. If you're running a contest, you need a prize that your target audience would love and then present the contest with graphics and photos. If you're taking a survey, you need to know what questions will draw your audience's attention and how the answers might benefit your company (hit their "passionate button"). You might even want to offer an incentive for responses. If you're posting photos or videos, you need to have them ready and sized to meet the demands of mobile users. You'll also need to test all links in advance to make sure they will go where you want them to and that they are working.

While you will want to post often, you'll realize in short order that quality content can get used up very quickly. Your social media team will need to have sources at the ready. If you have 10 people on the team, some will be engaging while others are scouring sources of interesting content, whether it's quotes, jokes, or the latest news story. Some will be brainstorming on how to educate and share your company's expertise and how to be helpful, while others will be positioning photos for your Pinterest page or editing a video for YouTube. It's a lot like a TV news broadcast: The lead anchors present the top stories while a team of reporters, editors, and production staffers are busy at work in the background, readying the content for prime time.

If, however, you are on your own, or working with a partner, you may need to have a simple plan of simply jumping in and engaging in conversations on the various platforms with your fans and followers, rather than continually posting content.

Finding Content

Social media teams use numerous tools and look for great content on a daily basis. They work hard to stay current. You'll constantly need source material, and a big part of your social media team's job is to follow both influencers and news in your industry, as well as to compile a wide range of content sources.

Content curation—that is, utilizing content from various outside sources—is often part of a social media strategy. Content curation directories and aggregators gather, organize, and provide content from a host of notable sources and sort them by theme or topics. These sites typically republish original content and link to the full entry, though some also provide interpretation and commentary.

Top directories such as Alltop.com can lead you to an extensive collection of blogs for almost any kind of topic, from numerous reputable sources including Mashable, Fast Company, and Wired. Then there are aggregators in specific categories, such as Inbound. org, Hacker News, and TechMeme for the internet marketing and technology fields.

Social media platforms also offer content opportunities such as Twitter Stories, LinkedIn Today, and the Explorer section of Google+ or the Google RSS feeds, which send you syndicated news stories throughout the day. You'll need software such as Feed Reader or

TECHNOLOGY BLOG DAILYTEKK.COM'S TOP 10 SOCIAL MEDIA SITES FOR CURATION

1. Storify.com. Building the story layer above social networks.

2. TweetedTimes.com. A personalized newspaper from your Twitter feed.

3. Keepstream.com. Organize your tweets with curation.

4. TweetMag. An app that uses your Twitter feed to create a simple magazine.

5. News.me. Your news from Twitter and Facebook.

6. MassRelevance.com. Social engagement platform of curated social content.

7. MyTweetMag.com. Curate content with Twitter.

8. Lynk.ly. News curation from your Twitter and Facebook feeds.

9. ChirpStory.com. Create stories from tweets.

10. Dashter.com. A WordPress plug-in that curates fresh content to your site.

News Aggregator for this or one of the many other RSS (real simple syndication) feeds.

Current events, news stories, and trends are marvelous sources of content, and commenting on news stories that are relevant to your industry is very valuable. And you can easily add links for integration across platforms. You want your customers or potential customers to follow you everywhere, so it's crucial to present content in a way that's specific to each platform. For example, if you run an animal shelter and a major oil spill is the story of the day, Tweet something about how that spill will affect wildlife. On Facebook, you might ask people to join you on your visit to the areas affected by the oil spill and let them know how they can help endangered animals and ocean life. On your Pinterest board, you might post photos from other sources, as well as your own photos once you arrive in the affected area. Then you might go back on Twitter to tell followers that you have new photos of how the oil spill is affecting wildlife.

You can also find content by doing a basic search for the top bloggers and top influencers in your industry or interest areas. A Google search of "top bloggers" will yield numerous results in many categories. There's also the Huffington Post, a vast source of content, with thousands of bloggers creating, compiling, and contributing material on a wide array of topics.

Rules of Engagement

At last, it's time to engage. The platforms differ, but some general rules of engagement apply across the board. It all starts with the basic premise of wanting people to like you and your brand, and to enjoy engaging with you and/or your business.

Here are some of the rules:

- *Let your demographics guide your voice*, so that you and your team can engage with your audience in a way to which they will respond.
- *Understand what motivates your audience and act accordingly*. Studies show that the number-one reason people engage on

social media is because they will receive discounts or freebies. The number-two reason is simply because they find the brand likable. What discounts could you offer? How can you be especially likable to your target audience? (Hint: Know what they are passionate about and remember their birthdays.)

- *Be creative.* There is a lot of competition out there, so you need to grab their attention. If you can engage in a creative manner, people will respond.

- *Make helping people a major priority.* You can win over a lot of people and prove your credibility if you can help them solve a problem. Plus, they will share your help with others.

- *Show your passions.* You want people to see that you have interests and passions, business-related or not. You need to be ready to comment on discussions that you care about.

- *A little controversy can be good.* That being said, be very careful. Controversy can also blow up quickly and cause significant PR nightmares. It's a double-edged sword, so avoid issues that are potential firestorms, such as politics and religion, and employ both common sense and political correctness.

- *Listen carefully.* The only way to truly engage with others is to hear what they are saying. Social media is one of the most powerful data-gathering and listening tools on Earth.

- *Build ongoing relationships.* Many people reappear in the same groups, discussions, and forums, so make your presence felt in those same places.

- *Engage in conversations; don't dominate them.* There's no prize for the person with the most comments in the discussion.

- *Don't promote, sell, or spam people.* Instead, connect: Build relationships and friendships.

- *Handle negative comments with finesse.* Be polite; inquire as to why someone does not like your brand, products, or services; state facts; disagree politely; and never lose your cool. Most importantly, offer solutions.

SCHEDULING SOFTWARE

Let me preface this by saying that neither I nor my firm use or believe in automation. Social media is about being human and building connections.

However, if you're conducting a few social media campaigns simultaneously across various social media platforms, you may need to schedule certain content to run at specific times—especially if you are a one-person operation and can't be at your computer or on your mobile devices 24/7.

There are several scheduling programs that can both remind you what and when to post on each platform, and even do it for you. Among them are HootSuite, LaterBro, and Buffer, as well as Twitter-only software such as Future Tweets and Tweet-u-Later. But even though software can help make your life a little easier, take care not to automate your social media. You or your team must still engage and interact with customers, clients, fans, and followers in an authentic way.

- *Let others help you.* Ask people what they think of certain products, styles, or services that you may offer. Glean information, but don't be pushy or overdo it. Nobody wants to answer 20 questions. You can crowdsource, but you can also simply ask a question to get people to engage.
- *Demonstrate your knowledge or expertise.* But be humble; don't ever seem condescending or patronizing.

Tips for Each Platform
Twitter

Twitter mystifies people and even major brands. It takes a lot to get the most out of it and to give your audience the best content at the most opportune times. Here are some strategies and tricks from a mid-2013 study by Salesforce, a leader in social and mobile cloud technology. These strategies can result in extracting higher levels of engagement out of your followers.

BEST DAYS TO TWEET

Saturdays and Sundays see a 17 percent increase in engagement rate compared to weekdays. Yet only 19 percent of all brand tweets are published on those two days. Wednesdays and Thursdays have the lowest percentage of engagement.

BEST TIME OF DAY TO TWEET

Tweets published between 8 A.M. and 7 P.M. see a 30 percent increase in engagement rates over Twitter content published outside of that time frame, and this includes Saturdays and Sundays. Sixty-four percent of brands take advantage of this trend.

LENGTH OF TWEET

Tweets less than 100 characters have a 17 percent higher level of engagement than longer tweets.

TWITTER HASHTAGS

Tweets that use hashtags see twice as much engagement as tweets without hashtags. Most brands do not utilize, or properly utilize, hashtags. In fact, only 24 percent of tweets from brands studied used hashtags. There is a 21 percent increase in engagement when using one or two hashtags and a 17 percent decrease in engagement when more than two hashtags are used.

RETWEETS

Retweet rates increase 12 times when a tweet asks for people to "retweet" or "RT." Only 1 percent of brands studied ask their followers to retweet. Asking people to "RT" increases the retweet rate 10 times, and asking them using the word "retweet" increases retweet rates a whopping 23 times.

Pinterest

Pinterest joined the party after Facebook and Twitter, but it is growing rapidly due to its capitalization on our natural affinity for visuals. Pinterest also utilizes some of the best engagement elements of the other two sites, such as liking and hashtags. Pins, which are unique to Pinterest, are how you collect, sort, and save images into various collections known as pinboards.

LIKING AND REPINNING

Liking on Pinterest is similar to liking on Facebook, except here you can pin a variety of images or graphics and then "like" specific ones. Repinning is similar to retweeting on Twitter, where you take someone else's image and pin it—crediting the original source—on your pinboard.

PINTEREST HASHTAGS

Hashtags are used in a similar manner as they are used on Twitter—for searching topics—and again, you do not want to overdo it by putting hashtags on everything.

COMMENTS

Because there is no direct private communication on Pinterest, it's advantageous to hover over a specific pin and add your comments

---

POPULAR WAYS TO ENGAGE

◆ *Pin it to win it contests.* This could range from the best board on a specific topic to the best picture of customers using your product. Be creative!

◆ *Coupons.* Coupons can appear on your boards or on a board created specifically for coupons.

◆ *QR codes.* These allow mobile users to access your images—from a new contest photo or something new about your products or services on your website—on their smartphones.

◆ *Use food.* With 57 percent of Pinterest users interacting with food-related content, it is the leading Pinterest category.

◆ *Pin prices.* A 2013 study by Wishpond Technolgies showed that 69 percent of Pinterest users buy products they find on Pinterest, and pins with prices receive 36 percent more likes than pins without prices.

---

there. This is where you can be clever, creative, and start a conversation that leads to engagement.

LinkedIn

LinkedIn is a networking tool and differs from most of the other social media sites. Unlike Twitter, where you may have thousands of followers, many of whom you don't know, LinkedIn is more selective and focused on connecting users with people they know or want to get to know through a mutual connection.

PEOPLE RULE

While you can have a company LinkedIn page and profile, the platform is best known for networking with other people. Most of your engagement should be conducted as an individual, though your personal profile can link to your business profile.

POST STATUS UPDATES OFTEN

Status updates let people know what you're up to and are a combination of your business activities and some personal activities, such as something about a noteworthy industry event you attended. While many users check in on LinkedIn in the morning—so it's a good time to post an update that will draw attention—posting throughout the day can keep people abreast of important activities and keep you fresh in their minds.

ENGAGE IN GROUPS

Roughly 81 percent of LinkedIn members belong to one or more of the 1.5 million LinkedIn groups. While many people post links to articles and blogs, you can also start conversations by posing interesting questions, which typically elicits more comments and likes than just posting articles. Look for groups related to your target audience.

BE INTERNATIONAL

If your business can benefit from being global, LinkedIn is a great place to share topics; 64 percent of members are from outside the United States.

PHOTOS

A profile photo leads to more connections and subsequently more engagement. You can also now use photos to enhance your status updates. Remember, images and videos attract 40 percent more attention than text alone.

CONNECT WITH PEOPLE WHO HAVE VIEWED YOUR PROFILE

If someone has viewed your profile, reach out to connect, because he or she has already shown an interest in you. Thank them for their interest and then for accepting your invitation if they do. You may even start a general conversation, ask a question, or refer to a mutual connection or group. This is an opening for engagement.

Facebook

Facebook is the king of social media, with more than twice as many users as Twitter and Pinterest combined. Having started out as a "social" site, Facebook has morphed into a home for countless businesses trying to engage their audiences in hopes of increasing brand awareness, lead generation, and sales. The sheer volume of Facebook users makes it easy to reach out to your target audience but hard to handle the potential volume of responses. If you post, be prepared to respond.

COVER PAGE PHOTO

Make your cover page photo unique, entertaining, engaging, and/or distinctive. Keep it in line with your brand.

TAKE THEM BEHIND THE SCENES

Behind-the-scenes stories are in vogue, and stories, photos, and links to your YouTube behind-the-scenes videos can prompt engagement.

GIVE KUDOS TO THOSE IN AND OUTSIDE YOUR COMPANY

Did someone in your company win an award? Did your company-sponsored softball team raise money for a charity? Have businesses with which you affiliate shared any good news? Post good news about others, for example, congratulate the Super Bowl or Academy Awards winners, and people will respond.

INFOGRAPHICS ARE HOT!

Put together an infographic with some of the latest data about your business or industry and share it on your Facebook page.

GIVE INSIDER INFO AND DISCOUNTS

Just as behind-the-scenes stories/photos are popular, so is letting people know all about tomorrow's sale a day early and giving them a discount. You can even poke people with a reminder that they can get a day early 10 percent off if they act quickly.

ASK QUESTIONS

Questions on a Facebook post, or a request for input, generate engagement—as long as they're short. Short questions generate more than twice the response of longer queries, and questions with one-word answers are the most successful.

"LIKE" SUBLIMINALLY

You don't even have to ask for likes. Postings that use the word "like" get 240 percent more likes.

DISCUSS INDUSTRY EVENTS AND NEWS

Talk about your industry without using jargon and start discussions on news stories that may impact your industry. You might also run polls asking your followers' opinions on the topic.

THINK WATER COOLER CONVERSATION

People on Facebook engage as they would around the office water cooler, so be casual and friendly when addressing them. Hard-selling, condescending, or overtly business-oriented posts don't work.

YouTube

Since its launch in 2005, YouTube has grown into one of the top 10 most visited sites in the world, according to Alexa, the web analytics and ranking company. What started, and still continues, largely as a home for user-generated videos has attracted businesses worldwide. But to engage an audience, videos need to be exceptional in both content and quality so that they will generate likes, comments, and sharing.

THE OLD SPICE STORY

Capitalizing on its extremely popular TV commercials, Old Spice created 180 individual videos on YouTube in response to users who'd commented on the originals. The shirtless "Old Spice Guy," as he's known, sent the videos via Twitter to bloggers, YouTube commentators, random folks asking random questions on Yahoo! Answers, and others who had tweeted about him. Soon people were commenting like crazy in hopes of a response from their muscular Old Spice hero.

The result? One of the most successful interactive campaigns in history, with 40 million impressions in the first week and a 107 percent jump in sales after the first month.

So, what can you do?

FOLLOW OLD SPICE'S LEAD

Respond to those who contact you with something unique and entertaining. If you have star power, use it. If not, find some way to communicate your engagement on video.

BUILD A CAMPAIGN

They do it with commercials; you can do it with videos. A series of videos centered around your brand can have people coming back for more . . . if they like it.

TAKE PEOPLE BEHIND THE SCENES

As with Facebook, you can get great results going behind the scenes from YouTube, such as when Boloco, the New England fast-food chain, used videos to be transparent about where their meat comes from. Cassidy Quinn, their social media maven and vlogger (a blogger whose media content is primarily video), keeps up with customers via the comments and replies to create a company-customer personal relationship.

GET PEOPLE INVOLVED IN YOUR VIDEOS

People love to make videos but usually don't have a company that can share it with a massive audience. There have been a number of YouTube-based contests asking users to "make our next viral video" or create a new commercial, and companies have had some great success engaging their followers in creating their videos.

CROSS-PROMOTE

Use other social media platforms to promote your YouTube videos and feature feedback, because comments are read more frequently on Facebook and Twitter.

Case Study: Red Jumpsuit Apparatus

The rock band Red Jumpsuit Apparatus had enjoyed a rapid rise to success. Formed in Florida in 2003, their second album, *Don't Fake It,* reached the top 25 on the U.S. charts and was certified gold in 2006, while their follow-up album, *Lonely Road,* peaked at number 14 in 2009. But after leaving their record label, Virgin, and going out on their own, they saw only lukewarm response to their 2011 release, *I Am the Enemy.* Determined to make a fast comeback, the band took to social media to rebuild.

By the time they came to us to ask how we could improve their social media, it was actually a slightly more difficult question than the normal ones that get shot across our bow. You see, Red Jumpsuit had become extremely active on social media and were pretty good at it. They had task-specific band and team members with responsibilities for individual social media platforms. They posted every day, several times a day, and engaged with fans. They posted pictures, enjoyed making videos, and totally got and appreciated the power of social media and what it could do for rabid fans.

So after careful analysis, we came up with what we felt was their one biggest weakness, and that was a lack of crowdsourcing. The power of soliciting feedback and opinions from your followers can be spectacular. Crowdsourcing can make a fan or follower feel like his or her opinion matters, and it is a great way to turn a follower into a true fan. It's also an amazing way to find out what's important to your fans and what they want to see from your brand.

After just a month, and thousands of answers to a few interesting questions, such as "What is your favorite Red Jumpsuit Apparatus album, song, concert, or video?", we saw an immediate increase in engagement on both Twitter and Facebook. In fact, besides answering these questions, engagement simply rose very quickly as well. Red Jumpsuit Apparatus's People Talking About This (PTAT) number on Facebook skyrocketed by over 800 percent (see Figure 5–4). We saw engagement across the board increase with more page likes and many more Twitter followers, retweets, and replies. It was truly an outstanding response, and has continued. Their fans were hungry to share their favorite Red Jumpsuit Apparatus videos, where they wanted to see them tour, and what kind of contests they wanted to see them run.

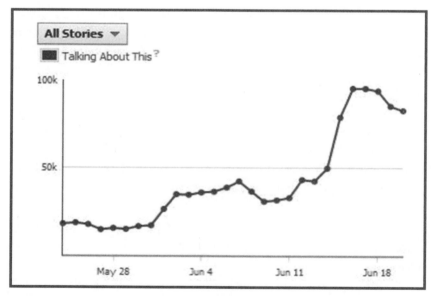

Figure 5–4 *Dramatic increase in social engagement for the band Red Jumpsuit Apparatus, just by crowdsourcing and getting their fan base involved in the conversation.*

In fact, shortly after crowdsourcing to find out what ideas their fans had for a contest, thousands of ideas flowed in, and Ronnie, the lead singer and CEO of the band, contacted us, stating that they loved the contest responses and wanted to kick off one of the ideas. Among their favorite ideas was to have fans shoot their own videos to a Red Jumpsuit Apparatus song or play instruments and do a cover of a song. This would then go onto YouTube.

At the point of writing this, the details of a contest and the prizes are being worked out, but it's safe to say that the band has been getting tremendous responses, thanks to utilizing social media and crowdsourcing. When you ask questions and look for new ideas, as in crowdsourcing, you get people to engage and respond to something they are excited about. You can also find some very innovative ideas. I've also recently been informed by Ronnie, the lead singer, that since engaging our company, Fuel Online, to fine-tune and improve their social media engagement, the traffic to their website has easily doubled, plus downloads and merchandise sales have increased dramatically.

Chapter 6

How to Build a Following

In this chapter we address the very frequently asked question by anyone trying to build a brand or increase their business: How do I build a following in the social media?

Get Out There—In a Meaningful Way

The first, and most obvious answer is to be out there, active and using social media often. It's like the state lottery commercials: "You've got to be in it to win it." The same holds true in social media; if you are not posting, tweeting, and making your brand or business visible on a regular basis, you are unlikely to benefit from social media. Like many other people, I have Twitter running while I'm working so I can check in to see what is being discussed or if anyone has a question or comment for me. I also check in when I'm not working. While you don't need to be available 24/7, you should be monitoring your social media platforms as often as possible. Mobile devices make it very easy to follow Twitter, Facebook, or any other social media site wherever you go.

Some people tweet more than 300 times a day, while others perhaps 25 or 30 times. I believe in posting content as often as you have something worthy of posting, not just for the sake of it. Some days I might post once or twice; other days it's probably 10 to 20 times. If there's something really interesting going on or I'm having active conversations my frequency of posts will be much, much higher. Your social media activities may serve different purposes: Some act as customer service tools, others as brand ambassadors. Don't place limits, but don't make meaningless and worthless posts.

You do want to respond to your followers promptly, which may mean posting often if you have many followers. While it's harder for a large company such as Pizza Hut to respond to everyone who tweets or makes a comment on Facebook, they can have a social media team trying to reach many of the people commenting and they can have answers at the ready to commonly asked questions. Most large organizations with social media teams are prepared with a list of frequently asked questions and their answers. Standardized answers are important, but make sure they don't sound canned. Try to maintain a personal touch by having your team respond personally as often as possible. When you're building a following for your personal brand or small business, it's especially important to both acknowledge them as followers—thank them or note that you're now connected—and to post as often as possible.

The Boy Who Cried Wolf

One of the most important aspects of using social media is having something meaningful to say. Don't be the boy who cried wolf—the boy who always sought attention for insignificant reasons but was then ignored when he really needed help. If you keep crying out for people to follow you, or you are tweeting or posting unimportant, meaningless dribble about your every activity and thought, you min-imize the value of your tweets or posts and hurt your brand building. People will simply tune you out. The head of products in a lawn mower company who is constantly tweeting about his every meeting, where he's having lunch, or each minimal change to every mower will not have much of a following left when he announces the launch of a brand-new solar-powered mower that could revolutionize the industry. The more you post or tweet, the more of a reputation you build for being inter-esting . . . or not.

Quality Is Job One in Social Media

In the end, social media success is all about making thoughtful com-ments on what others are talking or asking about. One great post will be shared or liked more than ten bland posts that say nothing. If people don't see something of interest in the first few posts or tweets, they may tune you out.

The public's reaction to television commercials is a perfect example of tuning out. Once you see a TV commercial, a billboard, or an ad a couple of times, you stop paying attention to them. This was one of the main reasons for the dotcom crash back in 2000. Dotcoms' business models revolved largely around the revenue from banner ads. These were initially static ads that appeared on a website's pages for any random product or service that offered the same message every time you looked at them. But because there was no research done on who actually visited those pages, the ads were often for products that the viewers weren't interested in.

At first, click-through rates for banner ads were incredible at 3 percent, 4 percent, or 5 percent—which drove up websites' revenues. Then they started to plummet all the way down to a minuscule 0.03 percent. Why? The banner ads were always there and always the same, so people tuned them out. The result was a huge drop in revenue for the websites posting them. Eventually, and not until after the dotcom bust, the idea of targeting ads to match the search became more appealing;

this way, if the user was searching something, he or she would at least get an ad that met his or her needs.

Conversely, one reason companies spend ridiculous amounts of money on original Super Bowl ads is to provide something new and hopefully memorable that makes you stay tuned rather than running to get snack foods. These original commercials have people talking the next day at the water cooler. That is what you want to do for far less money: have that same water cooler conversation.

The number one way to get followers is to give them something to talk about. If your goal is to gain brand visibility or to have people champion your brand, then you need to create and post content that attracts people who want to share what you have to say.

Share Your Expertise

A key way to build a following is to show that you are on top of the latest news in your industry, or even in national or international events, and are sharing your expertise.

Demonstrating your expertise without being a salesman is one of the more important tactical social media applications. It all starts with genuinely wanting to help people. Make it part of your strategy, or team member duties, to be helpful on a daily basis. Answer questions on topics that can benefit from your expertise with a reasonable amount of depth and help. If your response is going to be too long or in-depth, take it to email, but make sure the community knows you're helping and taking it offline.

Simply helping someone is a way to not only demonstrate your expertise, but to win over a brand champion. If you want to take it to the next level, you can start monitoring social conversations related to your topic or industry. For example, let's say you run a plumbing company; you will want to search for and monitor keywords such as "plumbing" or "leaks." When someone asks how to repair their leaky faucet, you can give some pointers. In other conversations, people may be sharing stories about what they have done to solve a plumbing issue. You can "like" those who have done a good job, while also offering your own story of how you handled a similar situation. Once people engage with you, asking more questions, thanking you for your input, or "liking" comments in an ongoing discussion, the whole world will see it. You're offering value and in return gaining potential exposure, fans, and business.

Selection and Editing

Quality content begins with selecting and editing what you are going to put out there. TV news programs cannot possibly air all of the stories that come into the newsroom, nor can a newspaper print everything that they hear about. When you are on social media, you are the media, and you decide what goes on the air and what does not.

Selection means determining what to tweet and retweet or post on your Facebook page, while editing means knowing how to say it and where to draw the line. How many people read five-paragraph posts on LinkedIn? How many skip to the shorter ones? Most of us. Editing is important throughout social media. Twitter makes it easier by limiting how much you can tweet at one time, BUT that doesn't stop someone from making poor choices of what to say. Bad tweets can be harmful because they reach a large audience quickly, before you realized you said something you shouldn't have said.

Even a simple quote or joke, which I sometimes post, is carefully selected. Why? Because you want a positive reaction. You want people to forward your messages or retweet what you tweet to their following to spread your business or brand around. This is how your engaging, enlightening, motivational, or amusing message gets out to numerous people beyond your own followers. It's your own—much cheaper—Super Bowl ad.

Retweeting

Retweeting is one marvelous way to utilize existing content and build your following and grow your brand. This is where you pick up on a message from another source that you feel your followers will be interested in seeing and send it out there.

For example, my followers know that even though I am a social media consultant and SEO expert, I am also a big NFL fan. So I might retweet a trade that just took place or a free agent signing with a new team. I'll give my followers information they may not already know so they can share it with their followers. If I'm retweeting about something in the news, I'll do so within 24 or 48 hours so it's fresh and still newsworthy. Old news is unlikely to prompt any retweets.

How does this help me spread my name or brand, you may wonder? Well, I don't simply retweet. Instead, I edit it or quote the original tweet. I then use the RT abbreviation, to show that I'm actually retweeting a quote of their tweet. It will say RT, but it will be coming from me and include the name of the original source.

For example, if an NFL commentator tweets about a trade, I retweet it to my following, so that they not only see the original tweet by the commentator but they will know that I sent it to them. I can also add a comment on the trade.

People can then respond or retweet the information to their friends—which puts your name, business, and/or brand in front of all of their followers. If you just retweet something without editing it, they wouldn't be retweeting your name and you wouldn't be connected to it. If half your 10,000 followers each retweet to five people, another 5,000 people will know who you are.

A good example of retweeting comes from a friend I follow, Kevin Greene. One day, Kevin retweeted a guy named Brent Hunter, who posted a quote, *"There are two ways of spreading light; to be the candle or the mirror that reflects it* Edith Wharton." Kevin liked it and thought he should share it with his friends, so he retweeted it as something he wanted to share. The beginning of Kevin's tweet reads: "RT@Brent Hunter" followed by the actual quote, so now all of Kevin's followers see Brent's name along with the person who sent the quote out and the person who is being quoted.

You can credit the tweet's author by simply leaving their name in the tweet, but to build your following, quote the tweet, instead of

> **Scott Levy**
> @FuelOnline
>
> Hard to know what to speculate on these days RT @Forbes: The gold crash is crushing gold mining stocks bit.ly/1562GQN
>
> ← Reply 🗑 Delete ★ Favorite ••• More

Figure 6–1 *Example of a retweet. Edit your retweets, @ the source and include "RT" for maximum effect.*

just hitting retweet, and your name appears as well. People make a big mistake of just hitting retweet—which doesn't do you any good.

If you look at Facebook, LinkedIn, and other social media platforms, you will also notice that many people are doing the same thing by posting and/or liking an article, a quote, or something of interest from another source. You see the author of the material and the name of the person who posted it, often suggesting a comment, a quote, or news that may interest you, as in my tweet in Figure 6–1.

Looking for Retweetables

So, what do you retweet? First, determine how much of your tweets, Facebook posts, LinkedIn posts, and YouTube videos will be about business and how many will be about other interesting items that may draw a reaction from your followers or friends. Quotes, trivia, jokes, company activities such as community projects, etc., are examples of nonbusiness content that can lead to brand building. Some people recommend a 4:1 ratio, with only 20 percent of their tweets or posts being about their product or service (although this won't work on LinkedIn where almost anything shared in the discussion groups must be topic related). I prefer a 50/50 split, although that may vary depending on your industry and your audience. Some industries have "breaking news" more often than others. It also depends on how you present the

WHAT ARE TWITTER CLIENTS?

Twitter clients are platforms or apps that expand your Twitter possibilities. They can help you manage your accounts and integrate with other platforms, such as Facebook. They can also expand the power of Twitter by displaying multiple columns side by side, each with a different focus, letting you see a variety of feeds and stay more closely connected to what's going on in the world around you 24/7. Two of the most popular are HootSuite and TweetDeck (see Figure 6–2).

Figure 6–2 *Various Twitter feeds coming in at once, displayed via TweetDeck.*

material. You can talk about your business without talking about it. For example, a gardener can provide phrases, quotes, and tips about gardening without discussing his actual gardening business or his services offered. On occasion, he might identify that his expertise comes from working as a gardener for years, but he shouldn't do this often or it might appear that he is self-promoting or even spamming. Typically it's best to simply provide expertise and let people find out more about what you do in your profile.

Among the most significant sources of retweetable material are industry experts—even if they are outside your own industry. For example, I am a follower of Adam Schefter, an NFL correspondent and reporter for ESPN. Schefter is an NFL insider; he has personal relationships with players, coaches, and general managers. When he tweets, it is typically breaking news, or the inside information that other reporters are looking for; in fact, most of them follow him. He has a massive following of more than two million people. This can lead to thousands, if not millions, of retweets. If I quickly retweet his tweet under my name, perhaps with my own comment attached, then I am providing news to my followers that they most likely haven't yet seen. I am breaking new information, possibly starting a conversation with my comment, and giving followers something they can retweet to their following with my name attached. So if my following is more than 250,000 and they retweet to an average of one person each, I've now reached out to half a million people with a message. Those who don't know me may then look at my profile to find out who this Scott guy is. And they can also retweet to their followers, which is what going viral is all about.

While the NFL is not my industry, it is something I am passionate about and so are many of my followers. I'm sharing nonbusiness information by sharing football news with sports fans who can get to know me better as a person (transparency).

Who to Retweet

You also want to follow experts within your own industry. For example, if you are in the health industry, you'll want to have relationships with the journalists who write about health and/or fitness. Perhaps you'll know someone at a pharmaceutical company or an herbalist with great inside tips for treating various conditions. If you're in the technology industry, you'll want to have relationships with the people at Google, Samsung, other tech companies, and tech magazines so you can get information before it is widely released everywhere. Also follow other people who are simply on top of the industry, trendsetters and leaders in the field. These are known in social media as influencers. If, for example, you are in the fashion industry, follow the top designers and fashion journalists. Every industry has its leaders who stay on top of their activities.

Influencers are people who, as the title would imply, influence others. They are the "thought leaders" in their industries and are on top of the latest news, trends, and ideas, which they convey often. They may be significant in publishing such as Arianna Huffington, perhaps a travel and leisure expert and blogger like Ann Tran, or a Facebook marketing whiz, such as Mari Smith. The point is, people often retweet them, or share their Facebook posts. I've seen influencers with 3,500 followers and some with a million. It's not about how many people follow them but about how influential they are in getting others to take action, whether that means following a trend, rethinking a social or political position, or even buying a product or using a service. In essence, influencers are akin to the wise village elders of ancient times whom people sought for their wisdom.

Accentuate the Positive

You'll also find that in a world filled with negativity, especially when you read the daily news stories, positivism can be very effective. People like inspiration that talks about success, business, their job, and relationships. Material about the "light at the end of the tunnel "or "turning over a new leaf" can be very motivational. I can't tell you how many times a motivational quote has prompted thanks from many people for brightening their day. Inspirational and motivational material can inspire people and touch their hearts so they not only appreciate it, but are apt to share it with their friends because they think it will brighten their days as well. Whether it's a quote from Abraham Lincoln, Mother Teresa, Oprah, or someone else in pop culture, if it is touching and meaningful, it can be a very effective way to spread your name, business, and brand.

Educate, Illuminate, and Make 'Em Smile

You'll also find offbeat news and trivia from within your industry may not be widely shared but is unique enough to retweet. I call it looking for that "Wow! I didn't know that" moment. A lawyer, for example, might post odd, outdated laws that are still on the books but make no sense in today's world.

Humor is always wonderful, provided it's not offensive, vulgar, or something that everyone's heard 1,000 times before. Be selective. I like corny one-liners that make people laugh, even if they know they are silly. You may find industry-related humor or something newsworthy. If it's a quote from a celebrity such as Letterman, Leno, or Bill Maher, retweet, always keeping the source. If you can find something topical and/or current, all the better, but, be careful and don't be too controversial.

Your industry's trade magazines, blogs, and newsletters can be a great source of information. If you can stay ahead of the pack and are privy to news before most others in your industry, you will gain followers, especially on Twitter where people go for the latest updates.

Knowing what is "trending" is also important. In every industry there are hot new developments and trends. Knowing about and staying

---

SOCIAL BAIT

I use what I call social bait to get people's attention on Twitter. This means tweeting something wild, interesting, or controversial (without getting in trouble) or a hot newsworthy topic that garners retweets. Every time you can bait someone into retweeting your material, they're promoting you. So if 2,000 of your 5,000 followers retweet it, then you've reached 7,000 people. That is how you grow a following: people spreading the word for you.

on top of them, from any and all sources in your industry, can put you at a significant advantage and will have people liking you on Facebook or following you on Twitter.

Your Following, Like Rome, Isn't Built in a Day

I have upward of 250,000 followers on Twitter. It's taken more than three years of hard work to build that following. Not only do you need to utilize the social media, but you also need to use other avenues to promote yourself.

I market myself at speaking engagements, always letting people know they can follow me on Twitter. You can do the same with your Facebook page. If I have an article published on Entrepreneur.com or in *Forbes*, I will list my Twitter handle and, if possible, my Facebook page. Your blogs, website, mailings, emails, newsletters, brochures, fliers, business cards—some people even put a quick response code on their business cards—and marketing/promotional materials should all include your Twitter handle, Facebook page, and any other form of social media you use. Your email signature can also have your social media contact info. And it doesn't hurt to get people you know to mention you and your social media connections in their blogs, articles, and at their seminars. Return the favor when you can.

While the other forms of social media can be beneficial in various ways, the two that can most help you build a larger audience are Twitter, because you can reach out to many people very quickly, and Facebook, because it is omnipresent: Almost everyone has a Facebook page. There are niches and scenarios, though, where some of the other platforms may be of more value to you. For example, you may use Pinterest when you have some great visuals, or LinkedIn, depending on what you do for a living or who you are trying to reach. Market your Twitter handle and Facebook page far and wide.

It will take time, but it will work. My platform of choice is Twitter, but I also use Facebook. While I have two platforms that I focus on, my firm must know the ins and outs of every platform, because our clients' needs vary. Understanding who you can reach and the positives and negatives of a social media platform is critical to saving time and money while getting yourself (or a client) the best ROI. For more on the other platforms and how they can serve you as a business owner, see Chapter 1.

Drill Down

Each of the major forms of social media allows you to narrow down your field to reach your "target audience." On Twitter, you can search by using keywords and hashtags that will link to conversations in your industry for possible opportunities to engage people. So if I'm in the coffee industry, I can find out who is talking about the topic and tweet that "I found a great blend from the northwest region of Colombia."

I also monitor the social media hashtags on Twitter to find appropriate conversations. Hashtags in your tweets will also help other people find you and the topics that you are talking about. It's a great way to let others who are searching for a topic know that you are tweeting on that very subject and likely to be tweeting on it again. Calling out to people who are interested in what you have to say, and are very likely to follow you, is a great way to build your following.

Be a Part of the Community

Almost every social media site has some form of community: the groups on LinkedIn, fan pages on Facebook, and Tweet chats. These are ways to monitor what people are saying about your industry or topics of interest, as well as an opportunity to join in, or start a conversation. The groups and fan pages are pretty self-explanatory. They allow for discussions or promotions and can help you meet people, connect, or engage.

Tweet chats are a bit more mysterious. They use a predetermined #hashtag appended to the tweets so that people can track them or search for them. By conducting a few internet searches, you can find a ton of great info and helpful sites. There are many websites that list tweet chats and the weekly or monthly schedules. Some only display live tweets from the tweet chat based on the usage of the hashtag. These will even automatically append your proper hashtag to your tweets if you tweet via those sites. It's a great way to meet others, network, and continue to establish yourself as a topic expert.

How Many Followers Should You Seek?

While some large, national companies, like McDonald's, are happy to have followers from anywhere and everywhere, smaller, niche businesses can benefit greatly from reaching people and growing a following in their own industry. A small business in a specific town, city, or region, such as a spa that can only serve 50 people a week, may benefit more from a select local following than a mass following of 100,000 people from all over the world that it could never accommodate. You need to decide whether your strategy is to build local leads, a national following, or international branding and visibility. I personally would rather have the followers than not. They lead to great random conversations, leads, and the sharing of my content, which is crucial. Plus, I never know who can be beneficial down the road.

However, other brand managers have different strategies. Many people on platforms such as Facebook or LinkedIn have found value in being selective in building their fan base or connections. Some simply don't want to share with those they don't know and feel may be critical of their brands; others are leery of connecting with competitors. And there are those who find themselves distracted by people constantly trying to sell themselves or their services, or who simply want to carry on meaningless conversations.

It's important to keep a few things in mind when building a following:

- *Your potential reach as a business.* Are you trying to brand locally or internationally?
- *Your resources.* How much time and money do you have to monitor—or have your staff monitor—your social media activities and interact with followers? If you have numerous followers on Twitter or connections on LinkedIn but have no time (or interest) in responding to them, you'll lose them as brand supporters.

TEN EASY WAYS TO BUILD A FOLLOWING

1. *Have an excellent photo, bio, and profile.* Every form of social media lets you provide some information about yourself. Make sure your profiles and bios include a succinct mix of who you are and what you do, but do not sell! Your photo should be a nice close-up of you alone—preferably sporting a smile. Make sure the photo is clear and close; if it was taken from 50 feet away, your face will look like a dot on mobile devices. And leave the photos of your family and friends to your Facebook photo album.

2. *Cross-promote.* Let people on Facebook have your Twitter handle, and people on Twitter find your Facebook page. Do the same on LinkedIn and other social media sites. A recent LinkedIn thread in a networking discussion group simply asked everyone to share their Twitter handles—and they did.

3. *Put your Twitter handle and Facebook page URL everywhere.* Don't be shy about letting everyone know where you can be found on social media. Some folks even have bumper stickers with their Twitter handles on them. Are personalized license plates next?

4. *Reciprocate.* If they like you, like them; if they follow you, follow them; and if they endorse you, endorse them.

5. *Be human.* Use your own identity rather than your brand or logo. On Twitter, very often the people behind the business have more followers than their businesses. You can also link your business page on Facebook to your own webpage. Also connect with the people behind other businesses; this can help you establish a relationship and you can even talk about, like, and cross-promote each other's companies.

6. *Use photos.* Yes, on Pinterest you will certainly be using photos. But they can be effective on your Facebook posts and your Twitter tweets as well. Photos grab people's attention. Make sure they are good quality and appropriate for your audience.

TEN EASY WAYS TO BUILD A FOLLOWING, CONTINUED

7. *Pay attention.* Each social media platform is trying to remain fresh, new, and innovative. As a result, there are new options introduced, some of which can benefit you in your effort to build your following and grow your brand. For example, in early 2013, Facebook came out with their new "Reply" feature, allowing you to respond immediately to other people's comments. You may not use the many features each social media platform has to offer, but it's worthwhile to stay abreast of the latest development.

8. *Set up a schedule.* While you may monitor social media all day long, you might be in a demanding job that doesn't let you spend great amounts of time actually being an active participant. If this is the case, you may want to set up a schedule to carve out time for making your presence felt.

9. *Review what's working and what isn't.* No matter what platform you are using, if growing a following and building your brand is your goal, you'll want to monitor your results. If you are putting yourself out there and people aren't responding, you may need to change your approach. If many people are liking your business on Facebook but ignoring you on Twitter, then focus on Facebook, or vice versa. Use tools such as Facebook Insights to find out where your "likes" are coming from. (We'll delve into monitoring and tracking tools in Chapter 7.)

10. *Be interesting.* I can't reiterate this enough: If you are interesting and engaging, people will engage with you; if you are boring, they won't. Choose your posts or tweets carefully.

Building a following will take some work; the good news is, you can do it from your office, your home, or while sitting on the beach with your trusty tablet. Remember to tweet—or post—often.

The type of product or service you offer. If you're a software manufacturer, for example, you'll want to reach as many people as possible. But if you're selling high-end furnishings, you may be better served with a smaller following of top designers and those who can appreciate and afford your goods.

Revisit Your Social Media Goals

You'll want to look back at your social media goals—the questions posed in Chapter 1—when determining how to best build your following. For example, if you want to become a topic expert, you should focus on a following primarily from communities in your area of expertise. That's also true if you are looking for talented people to join your business. In this case, you will want to be more selective, especially if you are seeking people to work in your offices. Their knowledge of the subject and geographic location are both significant factors.

How broad a following you want to build when your goal is to boost brand awareness or growth, or revitalize a struggling company, depends on the breadth of your brand. If your brand reaches out far and wide, you'll want to engage everyone; if you're more regionally focused, you'll want to be more selective based on your location. Keep in mind that a larger following means you'll need to spend more time—and resources— responding to them. So engaging with people 5,000 miles away who'll never visit your local spa or use your plumbing service may be a waste of their time and yours. But if damage control is your priority, it doesn't hurt to build a large following just on the chance that whoever you are engaging with has heard something negative about your business and/ or industry

Determine how many followers are beneficial to your brand. Some people will want as many followers, friends, fans, or connections as possible to build brand awareness. This way they can engage with thousands of people, get answers to questions, share information and expertise, and reach people who can potentially become customers. Conversely, others will be selective about their followers, friends, fans, or connections when building brand awareness. They don't want to have to engage with thousands of people, get questions answered incorrectly, or reach out to people who will never become customers.

Chapter 7

Measuring and Monitoring Your Success

onitoring and measuring your social media efforts are essential to your success. Without doing so, you will have no way to determine whether you're making an impact on your target market or are on track to reach your social media goals. Monitoring is imperative and it must be a significant part of your social media strategy.

At Fuel Online, we use both high-end enterprise level tools as well as platforms that we built ourselves to monitor social media at a very high level and meet the needs of a wide variety of clients. The most important area we monitor is conversations. You want to know who is talking about your brand and what they are saying. Are the comments positive or negative? Are people happy or frustrated? Monitoring conversations is a great way to learn what you are doing well and where you need to make improvements. Maybe your customers and followers are all talking about a new product line that is catching on, or complaining about the changes you made to a longtime favorite. It's a huge benefit to businesses, which have never before had the opportunity to listen to their customers, potential customers, and critics. It's like eavesdropping at water coolers worldwide.

Monitoring conversations is all about listening, and in my eyes social media is 10 times more powerful if you listen and don't just talk. Very often, companies are so concerned with what they are putting out there that they neglect to hear what's being said.

Monitoring and listening is how you find out how people feel about your brand. At Fuel, we monitor pretty much what everyone out there is saying about our client's brands or industry. We track who is engaging, what they are saying, and whether customer service issues are being resolved. The more we listen, the more we learn, which benefits the client's brand.

The Possibilities

There is a mind-boggling amount of data that you can monitor, measure, and analyze. Information that was once compiled though surveys or focus groups is now available through a myriad of tools, with 1,000 times more detail. You can easily determine not just how many people clicked on your post, but where they clicked from, and then how many went to your webpage. You can follow their activities to see if any resulted in sales.

Among the multitude of data you can measure:

- The number of views, likes, retweets, comments, or any other manner of engagement on any social media platform
- How much of your content is being shared and from which platforms
- How much time visitors spend on your social media pages or your web pages

- The demographics of anyone who has engaged in any manner
- Klout or Kred scores, to see if any influencers have engaged or are fans or followers
- Which content is drawing the most attention—for better or worse
- How many people contacted customer service and whether or not they were happy with the results
- Which platform, demographic group(s), geographic location, and even hour of the day is resulting in the most views, clicks, or conversations
- Which content, and on which platforms, is resulting in the best conversion rates

Three Keys to Success

We have found that these three core areas are critical to social media success:

Monitoring Your Performance

This includes reviewing everything from the best times of day to post to how successful your campaigns are. Review when you're getting the most engagement, where your reach is coming from, and who is responding—essentially, everything your company does, including the performance of each individual status update, picture, and video you share. You can see what is working and what is not. Performance monitoring lets you know if the time and money you are investing in social media is paying off.

Tracking Competitors

How do you know what results to look for? Are 3,000 likes good? Are 5,000 followers a lot? How do we know what the numbers mean?

For this reason, we consider competitor tracking to be very important. There's nothing wrong with keeping tabs on your competitors through public tools and public information; you're looking at your market and seeing how your campaigns stack up against those of your competitors. Compare your efforts with those of similar-sized companies in your industry. You may also want to consider other factors such as geographic region or how long the company has been in business and engaged in social media. That's how you can best determine where you stand.

For example, if you're a small business selling TVs, computers, and other electronic equipment primarily from three retail locations and through your website, seek out similar businesses with a few locations and online sales. Don't compare yourself to Best Buy, which has a much larger budget for social media and most likely a big team working 24/7.

There is, however, also a reason to monitor larger companies, starting with those that are one size up from your business. You can see what they are doing and model your social media campaigns after theirs in hopes of moving up to their level. By monitoring a larger company, such as Best Buy, you can also get some great ideas for future campaigns.

Gathering Industry Data

You can learn a lot about your own industry by monitoring conversations about the latest topics and trends. For example, if the Coleman Company, which makes equipment for camping and hiking, monitors its industry, it will see which outdoor products people are most passionate about and which ones they are complaining about. Such data can help not only with social media marketing opportunities, but with sales and even future manufacturing plans. Industry awareness keeps your business competitive and helps you capture the brand awareness you need to succeed.

Point Values for Metrics

One of the most familiar means of measurement is the use of numbers. We apply numerical ratings to illustrate how we feel about anything from service in a restaurant to favorite movies. In social media, many businesses also use point systems, assigning points for each activity taken by anyone viewing their content or engaging in any manner based on how valuable they perceive the activity to be. For example, if someone mentions your brand on Twitter, you might give that mention one point. If the visitor tweets about your brand, that might be three points, and if he or she retweets, that might be five points. A "like" on Facebook might be one point, because likes are easy to obtain, but a comment might be three points, and sharing your posting might be five. You can create the same measurement point system for any platform.

Because sharing is the Holy Grail of social media interactions because it results in spreading your brand, you will always want to give sharing the highest point total.

Point systems are arbitrary and you may not have a definitive means of determining what 100 or 1,000 points means in your industry or for your competition. But you can use the point totals to track your own success over various time frames. You can, for example, compare the numbers from June 2012 to those of June 2013, which can be particularly significant if you are a summer business. Many seasonal businesses find it very important to track engagement prior to and during their peak seasons.

A numerical point system also can help measure the quality of interactions and engagement resulting from your content. For example, if you have 5,000 visitors to your Facebook page in a week and get 1,000 likes, that's 1,000 points. However, if you get only 3,000 visitors, but 400 have shared your content, that content-generating activity rated at 2,000 points. That higher-value activity—400 visitors spreading the word about your brand—could result in thousands of new visitors and more potential customers. The quality of interactions and engagement is huge. A numerical measurement helps you determine if you're doing everything you can to get people to share your message. If you're seeing low scores, you can try special offers, discount codes, coupon codes, or simply more engaging content to increase the value of users' engagement.

Know What You Are Looking For

Success at social media means different things to different businesses. Your initial goals for using each platform will determine which results will matter most to your business.

Another measurement might be whether viewers are using hashtags. My company has been asked to see if people are using hashtags in TV or radio advertising campaigns. For example, a major national radio show wanted to see how many mentions it got during its shows by giving out a hashtag. If the hashtag got a certain number of mentions in that period, the show would give out a prize, tickets, or do a stunt. We suggested that it instead use its own "at" name—for example, @ FuelOnline. Mentioning a hashtag doesn't allow people to find or follow you, but by using the actual "at" user name, the brand can be shared. As a result, the show not only had numerous mentions, but the brand was shared to a wider demographic audience. We also have done the same thing for nationally televised shows and series. The idea is if you're going to involve social media, do it right so that you reap the most following and buzz.

Perhaps your goal is to better integrate your social media platforms. If, for example, you have marvelous photos on Pinterest or a great video on YouTube, you want people to check these platforms out. If you see that your YouTube visitors are coming from Twitter and Google+ but not from Facebook, then you need to review what you have on your Facebook page and how you can use the page to better integrate with your other social media content.

You can also use monitoring to measure your content's effectiveness. TV advertisers have been doing this for years, noting the responses to various commercials and using themes and characters that generated the best response in future commercials. Running the same content on several platforms can also help you determine which platform yields the best response from your target market. In some instances, reviewing the data may even uncover a new audience that you hadn't yet accounted for. You can then redirect your content to meet the needs of this new audience.

FOLLOW THAT LINK

Tracking a link can be extremely helpful when monitoring your social media success. You can create a specific link for any post or comment on any platform that will allow you to see where your visitors are coming from. For example, you can post a link on Twitter that is specific to that Twitter post to determine who came to your website or followed you to another social media platform from that specific posting. You can then follow the thread from that post all the way to your new visitor and, potentially, new customer.

Conversion

Conversion is a significant metric to track. Conversion is defined as the number of visitors, usually illustrated as a percentage, who take or complete a desired action. Such conversions can have different meanings for different types of businesses. For example, a retail or ecommerce business will define conversions as making a purchase. For a lead-generation website, conversion means a customer has "opted in" and will allow the business the right to contact the customer again. A successful conversion is defined as someone who has registered their interest and filled in a contact form.

Conversions are typically determined by the action, or actions, the business expects visitors to perform. Customer service can also be measured by conversion: A customer's concerns were addressed and they received the solutions to their problems. Many business owners and social marketing directors spend a lot of time trying to find ways to improve conversion and conversion rates.

Conversion Rate

A conversion rate is the percentage of conversions out of the total number of visitors. By using tracking application software, you can determine the number of views and the subsequent number of conversions. Calculating the ratio is simple: Divide the number of conversions

---

INCREASE LINK CONVERSION

One way to increase conversion rates is to make sure social media followers who click to visit your website are sent to a landing page that leads directly to the product, service, opt-in form, or whatever action you want them to take. If you make the mistake of dropping people on your homepage or somewhere else on your website, you'll most likely lose the conversion. Rule of thumb is that you want the user to take the LEAST amount of actions to get to the final outcome.

---

by the number of total views, then multiply the result by 100 for your conversion rate.

For example, if you had 200 total views and 6 conversions, you would divide 6 by 200 and get 0.03. Multiplying that by 100, you get a conversion rate of 3, meaning you can expect to have 3 conversions for every 100 customers, or 3 percent of your views would lead to conversions. If you determine conversions by the number of visitors who sign up for your newsletter, then you would use the same formula, inserting the number of people who signed up for your newsletter.

Conversion rates will vary depending upon numerous factors such as type of product, price point, marketing reach, geographic location, market share, etc. You need to measure conversion rates based on your goals and your industry. If you are looking to sell $10,000 pianos, you will likely have a lower conversion rate than if you are selling a $10 item. You also need to take into account your cost for each conversion. While social media is less expensive than buying advertisements, you are still paying a social media team. Is it costing you $5 per conversion or $50 per conversion? How many conversions will lead to sales, and will those sales make the conversion rate worth your efforts? Only you can review your conversion rates in conjunction with your budget.

12 Ways to Increase Conversion Rates

1. *Motivate with discounts, special offers and perks* that are time sensitive so visitors need to act quickly.

2. *Post quality content that appeals to your target audience* on a steady basis.

3. *Test.* Try various types of content, including images and videos.

4. *Include customer comments, quotes, and testimonials* so that viewers will see that others like what you have to offer.

5. *Keep postings short and to the point.* Lengthy posts, cluttered pages, or too many hashtags limit engagement and, subsequently, conversions.

6. *Offer an email blog subscription or opt-in email* to keep your subscribers involved.

7. *Remember the 80–20 rule that says 80 percent of your business will come from return customers.* Sing the praises of your current customers, thank them, give them the inside lowdown, and make them feel wanted and appreciated. Happy customers lead to conversions.

8. *Great headlines.* No matter what the content is, use a headline that jumps out. If your conversion rate is not what you want it to be, change your headlines. Businesses have reported 100 percent increases in conversions by changing headlines.

9. *Track your competitors.* Any public-facing information is fair game and you can access such data to see what your competitors are doing to engage people. You can then strategize to do something better, or different, to improve your conversion rates.

10. *Use calls to action that cite the benefit to potential buyers.* For example, if you are trying to drum up orders for a cross-training book, don't simply post "Order Your Copy Now." Your call to action could also include, "Cross-training can result in a toned body and a healthier lifestyle."

11. *Make your call to action larger or bolder than other content.* Bright colors, for example, have seen better conversion rates.

12. *Make every step of a conversion as easy as possible.* Each step you add will lose conversions. Take a page from Amazon, and keep it simple.

Return on Investment

One of the most significant metrics to track is your return on investment (ROI). The goal of ROI is to determine how much your investment—in money and hours spent, manpower, etc.—is paying off. ROI is used by most businesses to determine whether their investments are profitable. It's a simple formula: First, subtract the cost of the investment from the amount gained from the investment. Then, divide that sum by the cost of the investment.

If your gain from an investment is $50,000 and your costs are $10,000, take the difference—$40,000—and divide it by the cost, or $10,000. Your ROI is then 4, meaning you are making $4 for every $1 you invest.

The key to accurately determining your ROI is to take all your expenses for social media marketing into account, so you can see how much are you actually spending to get visitors, fans, likes, followers, or conversions. Your expenses include how much you are paying your social media team; how much you are paying for computers and software; how much you are paying for giveaway items, and so on.

There is also what's called hidden ROI—intangibles that are harder to calculate. For example, how much is it worth to have a customer who hated your business accommodated in such a way that turned them into a steady customer? How much are free giveaways worth to you? How much is your video on YouTube that went viral paying off? There are many intangibles that are difficult to measure without more sophisticated tools and many hours of tracking, so try putting an estimated number on them.

You may also find that ROI can be best measured over time. For example, the social media efforts to build a personal brand for an NBA star might not pay off immediately, but does after a few seasons when he gets commercial endorsements. A TV station can first measure ROI by an increase in viewers. If the station runs a contest that goes viral and gets shared 25 million times, it may then see a 5 percent increase in ratings. It can then track the number of sponsors that purchase time on the station due to the higher ratings. That can determine the dollar value of the station's ROI over time.

Three Ways to Utilize the Wealth of Analytics

Monitoring your social media campaign and listening to conversations will allow you to improve your social media output. To make it all work for you, you need to evaluate the data collected. Among the most important areas you can improve your social media efforts are:

- Targeting your demographic audience
- Improving your social media content
- Responding to comments and customer service.

Demographics

One of the primary uses of social media metrics is to hone your demographics. The more data you are able to gather, the more precisely you can reach your target audience. This comes from reviewing detailed information on who is viewing your posts and what they like, dislike, etc. For example, Facebook Page Insights provides data such as the percent of people by gender who have liked your page, age ranges, number of fans by country and city. I'd love to see even more indepth demographic data from them, understanding your demographics and how they react to your content is worth gold. Social media is ever-changing, and you'll want to continually update your demographic profiles based on your metrics.

Content

Reviewing which content was most viewed and how long people spent reading your content will help you create appropriate future posts. For example, a wine company that catered to connoisseurs found that sales increased after changing the content on their Facebook page to include a known expert's comments on the quality of their wines. They catered to their audience who enjoyed wine culture and wanted to know more about the wines. A discount beverage dealer may instead use a 10 percent discount to improve the conversion rate. Assessing what content your demographic audience responds to and giving them more of that content can increase your social media success.

Numerous business owners have also changed their social media content to give people a closer look at their business or brand. Remember, transparency is still part of the equation. In many cases, they added more photos or videos and saw improvements in conversion rates.

Event tracking also allows you to examine your content and determine which pages, tweets, photos, or videos generated more attention and which didn't. A tool such as Google URL Builder will let you see which of your tweets or posts generated the most clicks and which of those clicks resulted in conversion.

Content is still king, and using the data to improve your content should be one of your social media goals.

Customer Service

By monitoring conversations and responses to your customer service, you can continually tweak the process so that customers have nothing but good things to say about your business. Modeling yourself after companies in and outside of your industry that excel in customer service, such as Zappos, gives you an amazing opportunity to win brand loyalty.

Having excellent customer service can put you ahead of your competitors. But you need to stay on top of response times and customer satisfaction to make sure your excellent service doesn't lapse. While it is important to monitor all of your social media activities regularly, keeping tabs on customer service should be done daily. Just a few dissatisfied customers can negate many satisfied ones.

It's Still All About Your Goals

The amount of data available is mind-boggling. So before you become overwhelmed by analytics, you need to go back and review your social media goals. Social media can be a huge waste of time and money if you aren't paying attention to the appropriate data.

Analyzing data is integral to your success. If you're a retailer, you need to know total sales numbers; if you manage a football team, you need to know how many yards your running back averaged per carry, per situation, the previous year. Social media poses an incredible opportunity to gather a ton of data and use it to your advantage, even if you use a small percentage of the available metrics. It allows you to pick and choose the data you need and put the pieces together to plan your future marketing, on and off the internet.

Yet it is amazing how many people in all industries have Facebook pages, Twitter accounts, and Pinterest boards, but neglect to look at the results of their social media campaigns. They claim they don't have time, don't understand the metrics, or simply do not believe they can be of benefit to their business. When people seem resistant to reviewing the metrics or don't see the value in them, I ask if they are listening to their customers or potential customers. They can't honestly say yes until they have a definitive means of hearing what these people are saying, and that's what social media data is giving them.

Many business owners and managers worry about metrics and data that aren't vital to their efforts. Often they will nitpick over insignificant details while ignoring the big picture. If, for example, you are adamant about changing the color of your Facebook page, but your target audience is on Twitter, you aren't paying attention to the data. Track the data you need and look at the analytics that best pertain to reaching your goals. If you do that, you can put the myriad additional data aside.

You need to make changes to stay competitive, just as TV executives move programs around on their schedule or cancel them based on their

Nielsen ratings. Social media campaigns can prove extremely beneficial for your brand, but you must stay current and use the data you have to make smart decisions.

The Tools

There are tools to track all possible social media data. Most are easy to use if you take the time to learn them, and many have both free and for-fee versions, the latter offering more detail.

The most useful tools are often those on the platforms themselves. For example, one of the simplest metrics that many businesses find extremely valuable is Facebook's PTAT (People Talking About This) score, which measures word-of-mouth marketing. It provides the number of individual users or unique visitors who have interacted with the page. The number, which changes often, allows you to determine not only how many people are interacting with your pages, but also whether that number is staying consistent, dropping, or rising. For small business owners who cannot afford a 24/7 social media team, PTAT is a very helpful metric because it is a cost-effective manner of tracking content.

A slightly more complex factor to understand is EdgeRank. Even if Facebook users like a brand, they do not return to brand pages often, if at all. So many businesses look at the impact of showing up on users' news feeds, and EdgeRank is an algorithm designed to help brands increase their news feed visibility.

To understand the algorithm, it is first important to understand what "edge" means. Edge is a term for every possible Facebook action: updates, comments, likes, shares, etc. The algorithm takes into account each user's edges and then measures the sum total of affinity, weight, and time decay in conjunction with each action.

Affinity is the number of repeat interactions, including likes, sharing, commenting, etc., that a Facebook user has with a specific brand. The greater the interaction, the greater the relationship the user has with that brand.

Weight is a value system created by Facebook to measure the various interactions. For example, a "like" is very common and will have a lower value than a comment, where someone has taken the time to say something about the brand.

Time decay measures how long the edge has been on Facebook. A new posting of any type has a higher ranking than something that was posted days or weeks ago. This is included to increase the value of the latest news, or postings.

Facebook uses these factors to determine what shows up in people's news feeds. Having current, engaging content that prompts users to comment and share results in higher EdgeRank scores for the content. This will have your posts showing up more often on their news feeds, increasing your brand awareness significantly.

Tools provide anything from simple tracking systems to advanced data management from multiple social media accounts, and knowing your social media goals and objectives will help you decide which ones to use. Here are just a few:

- *Backtype.* Both provide statistical data on your social media activity and offers an overview of how you measure up against your competitors.

- *Blitzmetrics.* Lets you monitor content from Facebook, Twitter, Tumblr, YouTube, and other platforms. Checks news feed coverage, and feedback rates and helps determine which demographics are most responsive.

- *Bottlenose.* Analyzes and provides data from real-time activities across numerous social networks.

- *Buffer.* Provides free detailed analytics and analysis across social media platforms.

- *Buzz Equity.* Free social search content tool to monitor social media conversations across various platforms, plus a pro version that lets you store the distilled data.

- *Carma.* Lets you review and evaluate your social media image, brand recognition, and message penetration through traditional and social media analysis.

- *Conversocial.* Monitors comments and customer service issues on Facebook, Twitter, Google+, and Instagram. Comments are sorted into positive, neutral, or negative categories and can measure such data as customer satisfaction, agent response times, and issue frequency.

- *Curalte.* Applies advanced image analytics to social media conversations to help strengthen campaigns for Pinterest and Instagram.

- *Facebook Insights.* Facebook's free built-in analytics tool provides metrics based on Facebook content.

- *Google Analytics.* Provides web, social media, mobile content, conversion and advertising analytics and reports.

- *HootSuite.* A social media management tool that tracks various social media platforms at one time with free analytic data; a pay version provides more detailed reports.

- *MediaVantage.* Provides real-time traditional and social media monitoring in a single database to keep track of what is being discussed about your brand.

- *NetBase.* Lets you monitor social media or specific platforms in real time to analyze your campaigns, consumers, and competitors, and engage or react accordingly.

- *Pinterest Web Analytics.* Pinterest's free analytics that provides users with data on reactions and responses to their pins.

- *Social Mention.* Free aggregator that tracks user-generated content in a similar manner to Google Alerts, except the focus is on social media sites; also provides email alerts on your brand, your competitors, or your industry.

- *SocialOomph.* Allows you to follow up on keywords, auto-follow new Twitter followers, track retweets or utilize the many functions for tracking your social media accounts.

- *Sprout Social.* Web app that tracks content and conversations across social media platforms by demographic measures, monitors trends in social engagement, and tracks customer service response times.

- *Talkwalker.* Monitors trends, your brand and products, and also identifies influencers.

- *Topsy.* Lets you search by location or keywords and monitors tweets, retweets, websites and blogs, and analyzes, indexes, and ranks content and trends.
- *TweetDeck.* A service that allows businesses, organizations, and individuals to monitor, manage, and schedule their social media marketing activity.
- *Viralheat.* Aggregates your social media traffic into a single stream for easy access, and lets you sort using various filters.
- *YouTube Insight.* Provides total views, their demographic and geographic breakdown and even how long people are watching your videos.

Chapter 8

Advanced Social Media Tips and Tricks

D o you want to be a Rookie or a Pro Bowl Veteran? The way you go about "tackling" your career is similar to being a rookie or a veteran. You can go through the day-to-day and remain average, or you can study, practice, train, and try to find every possible advantage you can over your opponents.

For me, these are simply things you must do to take part in everyday social media. To others, these might feel like advanced techniques and tactics that are at a higher knowledge level and maybe even desire level when it comes to doing social media. If you want to elevate your game and get the most out of your investment (time and money) in social media, then I highly recommend that you take it to the next level with these tips and tricks. When you have mastered these and are hungry for more, then engage with me via Twitter or other means and I'll let you know what else I've published on the topic or where you might be able to learn more to take your social media to an even higher level.

Facebook

Trial Run: Test Engagement for Different Times of Day

A lot of companies post on Facebook only during traditional business hours. But what if your constituents are mostly abroad? How about those night owls? Tap into your inner scientist and experiment by posting on your Facebook feed during different times throughout the day (and night). Different studies will point to different conclusions, but the truth is, results will vary depending on the kind of users your brand attracts. The only way to ensure optimal engagement is through old-fashioned trial and error. While I NEVER suggest anyone auto-mate their posting, if you feel like you have to, Facebook now offers a scheduling tool so you can deliver late-night posts without disturbing your own beauty sleep. But keep in mind that when a company makes a post, people assume that there's someone there live. If you don't reply back or address the issue because it was a scheduled post and you aren't ACTUALLY there, you look bad.

Let the People Speak

Launching a new product? Deciding on a new design? Ask your fans for their input and actually ACT on their feedback. Whether you ask them to vote on a new logo or product color, use their input to reason-ably guide the direction of your next business decision. Not only will it increase your audience's brand loyalty, it also helps you get a sense of what your fan base wants.

Take a Picture—It'll Last Longer

More importantly, pictures are shared more. In fact, one study showed that picture posts receive TWICE as much engagement as posts with just text or links. Fans' news feeds are constantly cluttered with friends and business pages, so including a photo or graphic with your content helps your post stand out. And you don't need an expensive camera: Download Instagram to your smartphone to instantly snap and upload shots to your Facebook page.

Be Your Own Biggest Fan

In order to fully understand the latest trends and fads on Facebook, you have to actually use Facebook outside of your business page. So if you haven't already, it's time to join the rest of the world and create a personal Facebook account. This will allow you to see how fans are seeing your own business as well as what the competition is doing, and how other users are innovating online.

Get Your Fans Off Facebook . . .

And onto your email list. By giving fans an incentive to subscribe to your email list, you can expand your touch points. Keep your Facebook content upbeat and FUN, while saving more targeted marketing and upselling for your email campaigns. The results will speak for themselves.

A Call to Action

Because you don't want your Facebook fans to visit once and then leave, place a "call-to-action" graphic on your page's tab. It can be something as simple as "Like Us!" with arrows pointing toward the like button. Make it easy for visitors to convert into fans by giving them every opportunity to add you to their feeds.

Hide and Seek

Make people want what you have: Create content that is exclusive to fans only, which will encourage visitors to like your page. This could be special product information, interviews, menus—whatever fits in with your particular business.

There are a couple of ways to do it (and it keeps changing) via existing apps of custom FBML (Facebook Markup Language). Easiest method I've found is to do a Google search for "Static FBML app."

Some of them have the built-in ability to provide exclusive content only to people who have liked your page.

Here's the coding:

```
<fb:fbml version="1.1">
<fb:visible-to-connection> information for fans only!
<fb:else> information for fans and non fans!
```

But Be Easy to Find

Create a vanity URL for your Facebook business page. This makes you more discoverable so that your fans can just go to www.facebook.com/yourbusinessname. Just go to www.facebook.com/<your username> to update your business page name.

Post Weekly Pins

Not to be confused with a Pinterest pin, Facebook allows businesses to pick one post a week to be featured at the top of your page. So whatever information you're trying to push each week, be it a sale or promotion or event, be sure to anchor it to the top of your timeline. It's very simple: Just hover over the post you've selected to anchor, click the pencil icon, and select "Pin to Top." These pins expire every seven days, which makes it a great way to highlight your most up-to-date posts.

Show Off Your Milestones

Facebook milestones don't just have to be about relationship updates or graduations. Highlight your company's accomplishments, whether it's an anniversary, meeting a fan growth goal, or launching a new product. You can create a milestone in the status update box, then fill in information such as date and location. And as always, be sure to add a picture with each one!

Twitter

Follow the Leads

Twitter isn't just about your tweets; it's also a great source for information on your competition. But don't just follow your rivals; follow your *rival's followers.* This will give you fresh insight on how to broaden your own following and what those people are looking for. It may even show you what your competition is doing better than you. With a little tweet tweaking, you may be able to get those followers to convert to your own company.

Save the Sales Pitch

Don't get caught up in using Twitter as a selling tool. Instead, use it to increase customer loyalty and offer valuable information for your followers. Overmarketing will merely leave a sour taste in followers' mouths, and you may even end up losing them if their feed gets too clogged with too many promotions.

Keep It Short

Posting links and content is a great thing, but Twitter users are all about brevity, so be sure to shorten your links by using a redirect service. http://bit.ly and http://is.gd are good ones to use, but there are other companies that offer additional services. Take a few minutes to do some research and find the best fit for your brand.

Reply with a Period

Twitter filters allow users to only view replies if they are following each side of the conversation. But by starting off your reply with a period, the post won't start with @, it will instead be viewed as a separate tweet and will be seen by all of your followers. Breaking grammar rules never felt so good.

Lose a Few Characters

Yes, 140 characters is the technical limit on Twitter, but all the cool kids are now only tweeting with 125 or less. Short, punchy tweets will grab your followers' attention rather than getting lost in their feeds.

Twitter + & = ???

Lose the ampersand in both your profile and your tweets: Whatever the reason, Twitter doesn't display the "&" sign correctly, so save your followers the trouble of trying to figure out what it says and just spell out the word; it's worth the extra two characters.

Cross-Post to Facebook

Kill two birds with one stone by connecting your Twitter feed to your Facebook account. Head to your Twitter profile settings, then go to the bottom of the page underneath your bio. It's an easy way to have your tweets post automatically to your Facebook feed.

A Picture's Worth a Thousand Tweets

I can't stress enough how important pictures are in any social media platform, and Twitter is no exception. Use Twitpic to share photos as part of your tweets. Snapping photos on the go? Download the Twitterrific app to your smartphone to post pictures when you're away from the computer.

Nobody Likes a Qwitter

Qwitter is a great tool that notifies you when someone unfollows you on Twitter, and even goes so far as to suggest potential tweets that caused them to leave. There are both free and "pro" memberships available, depending on how often you want information and how detailed you'd like it.

YouTube
Maximize Video Descriptions

Don't just use your YouTube video description to talk about the video content; be sure to share links to your website, Facebook page, Twitter account, and Pinterest page. And think carefully about keywords that will optimize search results leading to your video.

Keep It Private—at First

It may sound crazy to initially publish your video as private, but videos take a while to process even after uploading. That means viewers can see these low-quality videos, rather than the actual final product! Give your video time to process before you make it public; you won't regret it.

Annotate Each Video

YouTube's annotation feature helps you interact with viewers as they are watching your video. Add comments or links that will pop up at predetermined intervals. All of the timing and content is decided by you, making this a completely customizable function.

Extend Your Reach by Podcasting

Another way to cross-market your YouTube videos is to upload them on iTunes as podcasts. Millions of viewers tune in to podcasts daily, making this a great way target new audience members. There are plenty of free podcasting hosts and publishers, making it cheap and easy to give your videos extra exposure.

File Name Optimization

While you may be inclined to put the most amount of thought into your video title, YouTube actually weighs file names more heavily than titles. Giving your file name an optimized title is a quick, easy way to tag your videos in user searches.

Video Transcription

Here's another SEO tip to increase your video rankings. Add a transcription of your video's audio. It's actually quite easy once you've created the plain text document. Simply click the "captions" button, then click "Upload caption file or transcript."

Customize Your Channel Background

This is an easy trick if you've got even the most basic graphic design skills (or a few extra bucks to hire someone). By creating a customized background or frame for your YouTube page, you encourage viewers to stay on your channel and browse for other videos. Click on your username, then "My Channel." Then select "Themes and Colors" where you can upload your image.

Give Yourself Credit

Sharing is a big part of succeeding on YouTube, or any social media platform, for that matter. But what happens when someone takes your video and tries to pass it off as their own? While your video may continue to be shared, no one will relate it to you or your brand. So take a quick extra step by stamping your website URL as a watermark on your video. This makes it much more difficult for people to claim it as their own original content, and even if it is shared beyond your YouTube channel, your business gets some automatic marketing. This feature should be available in just about any video editing software you use.

Integrate and Embed

Videos take a long time to make, so don't silo yours on YouTube alone. Embed videos on your Facebook page and provide a link on Twitter. Your followers may only be active on one or two platforms, but that doesn't mean they don't want all the information you have to offer. Always make it as easy as possible to provide your fans with your valuable content.

Brand Your Channel

Just like any other marketing tool you use, your YouTube channel and videos should reflect your brand's tone. Be consistent with how you portray yourself so that viewers recognize who you are among the competition. It is particularly important to create a sense of cohesion among all of your social media platforms. Be integrated in every sense of the word.

Pinterest

Tag, You're It

It's not enough to simply pin your own images and hope others will repin. You must also actively engage with others by repinning content.

A good way to gain new followers is to tag the original pinner in the description section. All you have to do is add the @ symbol in front of their name, and they will know that you mentioned them. Let's face it, it's flattering to know that our pins are being used by others, and adding the small touch of specifically referencing the pinner is a great way to gain a loyal following on Pinterest.

Put a Price on It

Pinterest users are not just on the site to find inspiration—they're also there to shop. If you're selling a product, or even repinning products that are relevant to your business, be sure to include a price tag on the image because these pins get 36 percent more likes than those without price tags. So even if you're not selling your own products, think of creative ways to incorporate products with keywords that pinners will search for. If you're a designer, create a mood board; if you offer styling services, pin seasonal looks from online retailers. Think outside the box to maximize likes and repins through product pinning.

Search Simply

Pinterest search analytics are far less complicated than those of Google and other web search engines. When uploading original content, be sure to use strong keywords as part of the image's file name. So rather than keeping the camera's generic "IMG_4289," customize it to reflect what you are trying to sell, like "round_brilliant_cut_engagement_ring.jpg." Even if you're promoting a concept rather than a product, you can still use this SEO technique to your benefit.

Get Verified

Show pinners that you are a trustworthy source by verifying your business. It's a very simple process on Pinterest's website that simply confirms your website. Not only can users see that you are verified, it also gives you access to Pinterest's analytics, which can give you a lot of insight on what you're doing right and ways you may need to improve.

Speaking of Analytics . . .

Check out Pinterest's "Web Analytics Walkthrough" video, which shows you how to measure your metrics and conversions. You'll be able to tell how many pinners visited your website for your Pinterest page, how popular your pins are, and what is being repinned from your website. Knowledge is power; make sure you have the most information possible about what's going on in your Pinterest page *and* external website.

Focus Groups

Checking out pinners who follow your business can give you a lot of valuable information about your target consumers. By following these pinners and evaluating what else they are pinning, liking, and commenting on, you can glean detailed trends about your audience.

Visually Market Your Content

Even if you're not selling a physical product, Pinterest can help market your brand. Pin industry infographics, charts, slides, or other visual elements. Also be sure to use photos on your blog or website so that people visiting can pin those images as well.

Provide Useful Information

This is another great tip for content-oriented businesses: Pin ideas or products that would be useful to your target audience. Have you read a good business book recently? Pin it! Do you know a helpful YouTube video on public speaking? Pin it! Be a resource to your constituents by providing useful, relevant information and ideas.

Guess What This Next Tip Is?

Start a conversation in the comments section by adding a question to your pin's description. It could be as simple as, "Guess what this is?" or an open-ended question about your business like, "Tell us what you think about . . . " By giving pinners an opportunity to comment, you're far more likely to create an engaging environment. And while I'm on the subject, remember your manners and comment back. The goal here is to be a hub of interaction for pinners and potential clients.

Board Focus

Create boards on whatever topics are relevant to your business or brand and start pinning images. Lowe's, for example, has boards such as "Helpful Hints," "Patio Paradise," and "Curb Appeal." Seasonal boards are also a good idea, and be sure to more actively populate the current time of year.

For Analytics Junkies

If Pinterest's business analytics just aren't enough for you, there are a number of programs for businesses that allow you to track pins in real-time, analyze your followers, or even help you upload and schedule your pins in advance. Here are a few online resources for those who really want to catapult their "pinfluence":

- www.Piqora.com
- www.PinAlerts.com
- www.Pinreach.com
- www.HelloInsights.com
- www.Pingraphy.com

Resources

Websites Reporting on Social Media

CisionBlog—http://blog.us.cision.com/. The Chicago-based leading global provider of media relations software services, designed for PR professionals, posts ongoing blogs about the ever-changing world of social media. Along with providing the latest in news and social media trends, Cision also offers Cision Influence Ratings, providing influencer rankings, which can be found in CisionPoint.

The Content Standard—contentstandard.com. A leading resource for marketers, advertisers, and media experts, The Content Standard stays abreast of the industry, providing news and insights on content marketing, social media, SEO, and industry news.

DailyTekk—DailyTekk.com. Just two years old, DailyTekk tackles a wide range of technology from games to gadgets to apps to software to social media. Beyond reporting the latest news, DailyTekk consistently delves inside the businesses behind the latest platforms and products to provide more engaging content.

Huffington Post—Huffingtonpost.com/news/social-media/. While Arianna Huffington has gained influencer status on the social media, the popular home for news, politics, and insightful information is also home to many social media blogs. They offer up the latest news and wide range of views on what the many platforms are up to.

Mashable—mashable.com. Claiming 60 of their articles are tweeted every minute, Mashable is a "leading source for news, information, and resources for the Connected Generation." The New York company has built a huge following by providing insight into the latest news and views on social media and the wireless world.

Social Media Today—socialmediatoday.com. An independent, online community for professionals in PR, marketing, advertising, or any other discipline, the site boasts the "world's best thinkers" on social media. Included are: member-generated blogs, articles, and newsworthy content on the platforms, tools, and companies that make up the social media industry.

Other Social Media/Social Networking and Photo-Sharing Platforms

In this book, we've focused our attention primarily on Facebook, Twitter, Pinterest, YouTube, and LinkedIn, while also mentioning Google+. Along with these social media giants are a number of other successful social media sites, including:

Flickr—www.flickr.com. Started in 2004 and purchased by Yahoo! in 2005, Flickr is a photo-sharing site that predated the more popular Pinterest and Instagram (mentioned below). Some 6 billion photos are on Flickr, ranging from marvelous quality to overexposed or out of focus. It is about sharing photos for better and for worse and not about being an expert photographer. The photo community includes shared interest groups, photo tagging, and comments, and is popular for bloggers and social media users looking to include photos in their blogs and postings. Copyright rules are in place, but (as is often the case) there are still concerns about their enforcement, so it pays to read their policies before posting photos. Flickr offers both free and paid membership, with the latter offering unlimited uploads and bandwidth. Other sites notwithstanding, Flickr is still ranking highly for the average user looking to post photos.

FourSquare—Foursquare.com. An outgrowth of the increase in mobile technology and app technology, Foursquare is a location-finder and social network for mobile users looking to locate anything from a nearby Chinese restaurant to a place to buy a Scottish kilt. They can then share with others what they have discovered. Since 2009, the site has expanded from 100 check-in locations to worldwide check-ins and now features nearly a dozen languages.

Through their smartphones or other mobile devices, users can let their friends know where they are, write reviews and tips for the location, or make a list of places they want to check out. They can even go back and review their history of check-ins. Users can also post check-ins on Facebook and Twitter or upload location photos to Instagram. Mobile businesses, such as food trucks, have benefitted from FourSquare by being able to keep their customers posted on where they will be and when. Other businesses benefit from the word-of-mouth marketing that comes from users recommending a business to their friends who may be down the street and can walk right in. The platform rewards regular visitors with badges and by awarding points. Meanwhile, businesses may also offer discounts to FourSquare users who bring them additional business.

Instagram—Instagram.com. Launched in 2010, this photo-sharing and social media site grew to more than 100 million active users in less than three years largely based on its popularity and ease of use on mobile device platforms, including iPhone, iPad, iPod Touch, Android camera phones, and other handheld favorites. Web profiles include user info and photos that can be tagged and easily browsed by friends. It also allows for photo sharing across other platforms, including Facebook, Twitter, Tumblr, and Flickr. Instagram users can hashtag company names as well as products or services, which means businesses can see who is sharing their photos. As Instagram continues to capitalize on the mobile market, app makers have created a number of impressive mobile options designed to enhance the Instagram user experience.

Myspace—www.myspace.com. News of their demise was premature as Myspace continues with a revamped look and a media campaign to re-introduce itself to the public. One of the first social media giants, My Space (as it was formerly known) was founded in 2003 and peaked in 2008, reaching nearly $1 billion in revenue before a steady decline, prompted in part by the competition from Facebook, and in part by widespread media stories about security issues and sexual predators lurking on the site. Trying to grow too quickly and allowing too much freedom for site users were also reasons why the original My Space began to collapse.

Following significant layoffs and shakeups, the site has been reinvented, in part by its new co-owner, pop star Justin Timberlake. The new site actually began in late 2012 as a venue for promoting new music. Several artists such as Lily Allen, Owl City, and the Arctic Monkeys owed much of their followings to the previous rendition of the site, which had begun to feature new music. The revamped site, following that lead, officially emerged with a mission to combine the features of a social media site with that of a streaming music site, which, in this case, features playlists and user-generated "radio stations." Myspace now also features an app and is designed with tablets and phones in mind, scrolling horizontally rather than vertically. The mobile app also has a function that allows users to create and share animated GIFs.

Tagged—www.tagged.com. Sporting more than 300 million members globally in more than 220 countries, Tagged has grown into one of the world's largest social networks. One primary difference from other social media platforms is that Tagged focuses on, and encourages, users to meet new people, rather than building a network with established friends and business contacts. However, the platform is not a "dating" website. Tagged, which launched in 2004, also focuses largely on playing interactive games and sharing group interests. In 2010, Tagged was ranked 476 on *Inc.*'s list of top 500 Fastest Growing Private Companies thanks to an extraordinary three-year revenue growth rate of 632.2 percent. Tagged has also been named one of the ten best places to work by *The San Francisco Business Times* in 2011 and one of America's Most promising Companies by *Forbes* in 2012.

Tumblr—www.tumblr.com. Now mentioned right after the big six (Facebook, YouTube, Twitter, LinkedIn, Pinterest, and Google+) Tumblr has made significant inroads since its appearance on the social media scene in 2006. The site specializes in hosting microblogs from users. They can also post likes, comments, quotes, re-blog, or simply follow other bloggers. Like the hashtags on Twitter, Tumblr allows users to tag a post or photos from their own blog to help others locate it based on the subject matter. The service also has apps for iPhones, Android and Windows Phone.

Finding Influencers

Klout—klout.com. Klout measures user interactions on Twitter, Facebook, Google+, LinkedIn, Foursquare, Wikipedia, and Instagram to create user profiles that are assigned a Klout score. Brands working with Klout can also participate in a Perks program.

Kred—kred.com. Kred offers dual scores that integrate both influence and outreach. This provides an indicator of overall relationships and potential reach of a user. Kred also has a rewards program, giving away discounts and product samples based on users' scores.

Web Data

Alexa—alexa.com. Formerly a search engine, Alexa is a leader in providing web statistical information, tracking roughly 30 million websites. The San Francisco Amazon subsidiary tracks various metrics, including global traffic, and provides rankings, which include listings of websites by subject category or by country. Alexa also provides a free toolbar creator that allows site owners to create browser add-ons that engage their audience, which can help them drive traffic back to their website.

Social Media Glossary

Analytics: The gathering and analyzing of statistics and data to see patterns and improve upon social media, or web marketing, strategies.

Brand: The creation of an overall identity for a business that defines its products and/or services as well as the business's image, personality, and what it stands for. People become familiar with the brand and know what to expect from the products and services. Coca-Cola, for example, has a powerful and highly recognizable corporate brand that focuses on the strength of the name as much as the features of any one of the Coca-Cola products. Building brand awareness is a significant business use of social media.

Brand awareness: The concept of making consumers aware of a business's or individual's unique selling propositions. Greater brand awareness allows a company to have an edge over its competitors, and more sales (even with a similar service or product).

Brand champion: A fan or follower who regularly spreads the word about the brand, its vision, its products and services, etc.

Brand consistency: Having the same message, image, logo, tone, and style for your brand across social media, as well as traditional media, platforms.

Content curation: The use of content from various outside sources on your social media platform.

Convergence: The integration of several forms of media.

Conversion: The end result of the action you want your visitors to take, whether it is to sign up for a subscription or make a purchase.

Conversion rate: The rate of conversions, illustrated as a percentage, determines how many took the desired action out of the total number of visitors to the site. This allows business owners to determine how many of their visitors are doing what they had hoped visitors would do, rather than just visiting the site while taking no action.

Cross-promotion: The act of promoting your brand, products, services, etc. across various social media platforms by linking them together. For example, you may post a video on YouTube and then promote it on Twitter, Facebook, and other media outlets.

Crowdsourcing: The gathering of opinions, suggestions, or even submissions (such as a new logo) from the online community at large. Businesses often utilize the thoughts, ideas, and concepts of the "crowd" to make decisions about anything from new products to a new look for the website.

Engagement: Interacting on social media with others, whether business or personal, such as posting comments or sharing content. Any type of social media interaction is considered engagement.

Influencers: People who influence what others are using, reading, and talking about online. They are often the "thought leaders" in their industries and are on top of the latest news, trends, and ideas, which they frequently convey.

Infographic: A term derived from the combination of information and graphics, this is a visually engaging representation of information, data, and statistics.

Personal brand: The image/persona created and marketed for an individual. Athletes, celebrities, and major business owners typically have their own personal brands.

Profile: An online bio, typically with a photo, provided and updated by the user. Depending on the social media site, this may include business information, personal information, or both.

QR codes: "Quick response codes" are two-dimensional black and white square barcodes that can be read by cell phones and smartphones. They can encode text or a URL, or provide access to images or other information online.

Return on investment (ROI): The amount of profit you are seeing for your investment. In social media, this helps business owners determine the best ways in which to spend their dollars.

Sharing: Passing along information to other members of the social media community. For a business, getting followers or fans to share your content is significant and can help grow a brand, ultimately generating more customers. Sharing by followers or fans is essentially free publicity.

Tag: To link a graphic or text from an item to a profile or homepage. Tagging something, such as a friend's face in a photo, will allow that person's friends to see your photo, depending on the tagged person's privacy settings.

Transparency: Being open, authentic, and honest in what you present as content on your website, your profile, and your social media campaigns and engagements.

Viral: From the word *virus*, it is the phrase used when something on social media becomes "infectious" and spreads rapidly through sharing, or "going viral."

About the Author

Scott Levy is a social media and SEO pro. Founder and CEO of Fuel Online, he has been a consultant in the business since 1998. Scott is considered by many an industry pioneer and a thought-leader, and is often requested to speak at conferences and events. Always on the cusp of the latest internet trends, he also writes about social media and technology for a number of publications, including *Forbes* and *Entrepreneur*. Scott has also been interviewed by CNN.

A world-renowned firm, Fuel Online manages SEO and social media for a variety of clients, ranging from midsize companies to Fortune 500 corporations, as well as actors, athletes, and bands. Scott takes pride in his company's advanced, high level of work, continuously abiding by his motto, "Underpromise and Overdeliver."

Passionate about his business, Scott is a risk-taker who is known to pull no punches. When he's not online, you can find Scott outside, hiking, camping, or trail-riding his horse. An animal lover at heart, he also owns and adopts dogs. Follow Scott on Twitter @FuelOnline and see how he inspires people worldwide, motivating them in both life and business.

Index